INTRODUCTION

Distinctive Home Designs

Vacation Home Plans is a collection of best-selling vacation plans from some of the nation's leading designers and architects. Only quality plans with sound design, functional layout, energy efficiency and affordability have been selected.

This plan book covers a wide range of architectural styles in a popular range of sizes. A broad assortment is presented to match a wide variety of lifestyles and budgets. Each design page features floor plans, a front view of the house and a list of features. All floor plans show room dimensions, exterior dimensions and the interior square footage of the home.

Technical Specifications

At the time the construction drawings were prepared, every effort was made to ensure that these plan and specifications meet nationally recognized building codes (BOCA, Southern Building Code Congress and others). Because national building codes change or vary from area to area some drawing modifications and/or the assistance of a professional designer or architect may be necessary to comply with your local codes or to accommodate specific building site conditions. We advise you to consult with your local building official for information regarding codes governing your area.

Detailed Material Lists

An accurate material list showing the quantity, dimensions and description of the major building materials necessary to construct your new home can save you a considerable amount of time and money. See Home Plans Index on page 111 for availability.

Fax-A-Plan™

This is an ideal option for those who have interest in several home designs and want more information. Rear and side views for most designs in this publication are available via fax, along with a list of key construction features (i.e. roof slopes, ceiling heights, insulation values, type of roof and wall construction) and more. Just call our automated FAX-A-PLAN service at 1-314-770-2228 available 24 hours a day - 7 days a week. Use of this service is free of charge. See Home Plans Index on page 111 for availability.

Blueprint Ordering - Fast and Easy

Your ordering is made simple by following the instructions on page 114. See page 111 for more information on what type of blueprint packages are available and how many plan sets to order.

Your Home, Your Way

The blueprints you receive are a master plan for building your new home. They start you on your way to what may well be the most rewarding experience of your life.

D!... HOME PLANS

CONTENTS

House shown on front cover is Plan #X22-N147 and is featured on page 31.

Vacation Home Plans is published by Home Design Alternatives, Inc. (HDA, Inc.) 4390 Green Ash Drive, St. Louis, MO 63045. All rights reserved. Reproduction in whole or in part without written permission of the publisher is prohibited. Printed in U.S.A © 2003. Artist drawings shown in this publication may vary slightly from the actual working blueprints.

QUICK AND EASY CUSTOMIZING
MAKE CHANGES TO YOUR HOME PLAN IN 4 STEPS

HERE'S AN *AFFORDABLE* AND *EFFICIENT* WAY TO MAKE CHANGES TO YOUR PLAN.

1 Select the house plan that most closely meets your needs. Purchase of a reproducible master is necessary in order to make changes to a plan.

2 Call 1-800-373-2646 to place your order. Tell the sales representative you're interested in customizing a plan. A $50 refundable consultation fee will be charged. You will then be instructed to complete a customization checklist indicating all the changes you wish to make to your plan. You may attach sketches if necessary. If you proceed with the custom changes the $50 will be credited to the total amount charged.

3 FAX the completed customization checklist to our design consultant at 1-866-477-5173 or e-mail blarochelle@drummonddesigns.com. Within *24-48 business hours you will be provided with a written cost estimate to modify your plan. Our design consultant will contact you by phone if you wish to discuss any of your changes in greater detail.

4 Once you approve the estimate, a 75% retainer fee is collected and customization work gets underway. Preliminary drawings can usually be completed within *5-10 business days. Following approval of the preliminary drawings your design changes are completed within *5-10 business days. Your remaining 25% balance due is collected prior to shipment of your completed drawings. You will be shipped five sets of revised blueprints or a reproductible master, plus a customized materials list if required.

*Terms are subject to change without notice.

BEFORE
Plan 2829

Customized Version of Plan 2829

AFTER

MODIFICATION PRICING GUIDE

CATEGORIES	Average Cost from...	to
Adding or removing living space (square footage)	Quote required	
Adding or removing a garage	$400	$680
Garage: Front entry to side load or vice versa	Starting at $300	
Adding a screened porch	$280	$600
Adding a bonus room in the attic	$450	$780
Changing full basement to crawl space or vice versa	Starting at $220	
Changing full basement to slab or vice versa	Starting at $260	
Changing exterior building material	Starting at $200	
Changing roof lines	$360	$630
Adjusting ceiling height	$280	$500
Adding, moving or removing an exterior opening	$55 per opening	
Adding or removing a fireplace	$90	$200
Modifying a non-bearing wall or room	$55 per rooom	
Changing exterior walls from 2"x4" to 2"x6"	Starting at $200	
Redesigning a bathroom or a kitchen	$120	$280
Reverse plan right reading	Quote required	
Adapting plans for local building code requirements	Quote required	
Engineering stamping only	$450 / any state	
Any other engineering services	Quote required	
Adjust plan for handicapped accessibility	Quote required	
Interactive illustrations (choices of exterior materials)	Quote required	
Metric conversion of home plan	$400	

Note: Any home plan can be customized to accommodate your desired changes. The average prices specfied above are provided only as examples for the most commonly requested changes, and are subject to change without notice. Prices for changes will vary according to the number of modifications requested, plan size, style, and metod of design used by the original designer. To obtain a detailed cost estimate, please contact us.

Small Home Is Remarkably Spacious

SPECIAL FEATURES

- 914 total square feet of living area
- Large porch for leisure evenings
- Dining area with bay window, open stair and pass-through kitchen creates openness
- Basement includes generous garage space, storage area, finished laundry and mechanical room
- 2 bedrooms, 1 bath, 2-car drive under garage
- Basement foundation

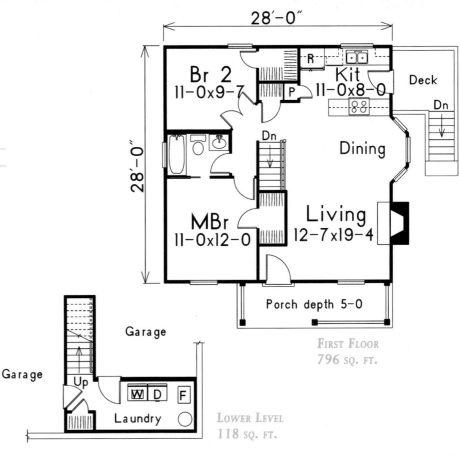

FIRST FLOOR
796 SQ. FT.

LOWER LEVEL
118 SQ. FT.

Enchanting Country Cottage

SPECIAL FEATURES

- 1,140 total square feet of living area,

- Open and spacious living and dining areas for family gatherings

- Well-organized kitchen with an abundance of cabinetry and a built-in pantry

- Roomy master bath features double-bowl vanity

- 3 bedrooms, 2 baths, 2-car drive under garage

- Basement foundation

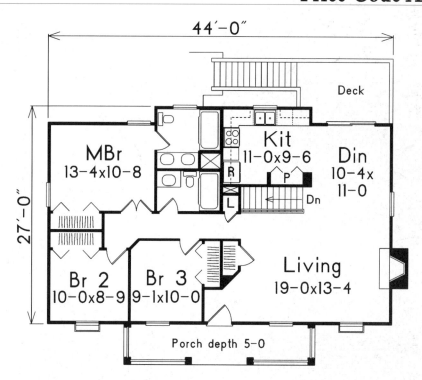

Atrium Living For Views On A Narrow Lot

SPECIAL FEATURES

- 1,231 total square feet of living area

- Dutch gables and stone accents provide an enchanting appearance for a small cottage

- The spacious living room offers a masonry fireplace, atrium with window wall and is open to a dining area with bay window

- A breakfast counter, lots of cabinet space and glass sliding doors to a walk-out balcony create a sensational kitchen

- 2 bedrooms, 2 baths, 1-car drive under garage

- Walk-out basement foundation 380 square feet of optional living area on the lower level

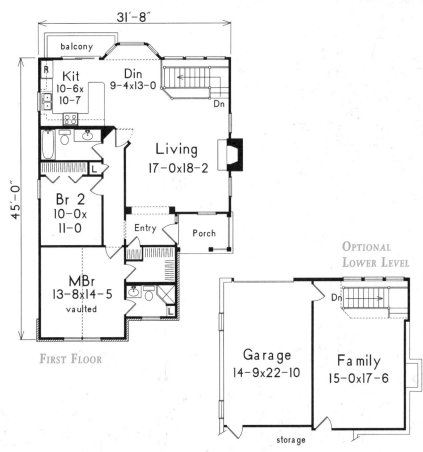

Apartment Garage With Surprising Interior

SPECIAL FEATURES

- 632 total square feet of living area
- Porch leads to vaulted entry and stair with feature window, coat closet and access to garage/laundry
- Cozy living room offers vaulted ceiling, fireplace, large palladian window and pass-through to kitchen
- A garden tub with arched window is part of a very roomy bath
- 1 bedroom, 1 bath, 2-car garage
- Slab foundation

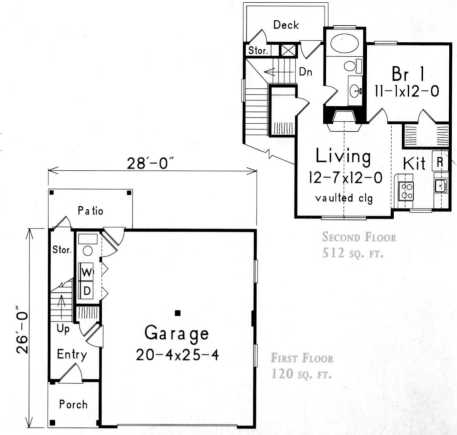

SECOND FLOOR
512 SQ. FT.

FIRST FLOOR
120 SQ. FT.

Spacious A-Frame

SPECIAL FEATURES

- 1,769 total square feet of living area
- Living room boasts elegant cathedral ceiling and fireplace
- U-shaped kitchen and dining area combine for easy living
- Secondary bedrooms include double closets
- Secluded master bedroom with sloped ceiling, large walk-in closet and private bath
- 3 bedrooms, 2 baths
- Basement foundation, drawings also include crawl space and slab foundations

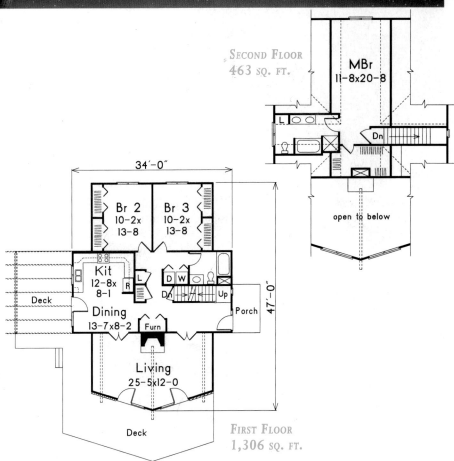

REAR VIEW

Tranquility Of
An Atrium Cottage

SPECIAL FEATURES

- 1,384 total square feet of living area
- Wrap-around country porch for peaceful evenings
- Vaulted great room enjoys a large bay window, stone fireplace, pass-through kitchen and awesome rear views through atrium window wall
- Master suite features double entry doors, walk-in closet and a fabulous bath
- Atrium open to 611 square feet of optional living area below
- 2 bedrooms, 2 baths, 1-car side entry garage
- Walk-out basement foundation

Family Rm
25-0x21-4

Up
Patio

Unexcavated

Unfinished Basement

OPTIONAL
LOWER LEVEL

55'-8"

Atrium below

Dn
Dining Area

Kit
10-2x
11-9

Garage
22-0x11-9

Great Rm
18-0x21-8
vaulted

Laundry
D W
R

46'-0"

Cover porch depth 6-0

Br 2
11-4x12-6

MBr
12-8x15-0

FIRST FLOOR
1,384 SQ. FT.

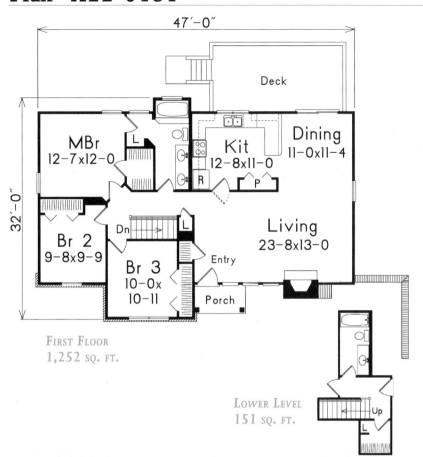

47'-0"

32'-0"

Deck

MBr
12-7x12-0

L

Kit
12-8x11-0

Dining
11-0x11-4

R

P

Br 2
9-8x9-9

Dn

L

Living
23-8x13-0

Br 3
10-0x
10-11

Entry

Porch

FIRST FLOOR
1,252 SQ. FT.

LOWER LEVEL
151 SQ. FT.

Up

L

Summer Home
Or Year-Round

SPECIAL FEATURES

- 1,403 total square feet of living area

- Impressive living areas for a modest-sized home

- Special master/hall bath has linen storage, step-up tub and lots of window light

- Spacious closets everywhere you look

- 3 bedrooms, 2 baths, 2-car drive under garage and second bath on lower level

- Basement foundation

Trendsetting Appeal
For A Narrow Lot

SPECIAL FEATURES

- 1,294 total square feet of living area
- Great room features fireplace and large bay with windows and patio doors
- Enjoy a laundry room immersed in light with large windows, arched transom and attractive planter box
- Vaulted master bedroom with bay window and walk-in closets
- Bedroom #2 boasts a vaulted ceiling, plant shelf and half bath, perfect for a studio
- 2 bedrooms, 1 full bath, 2 half baths, 1-car rear entry garage
- Basement foundation

FIRST FLOOR
718 SQ. FT.

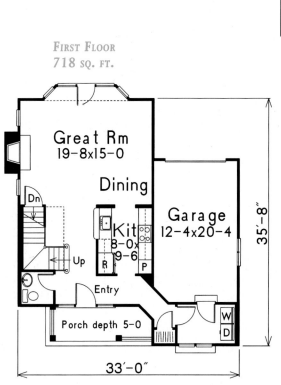

SECOND FLOOR
576 SQ. FT.

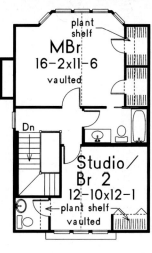

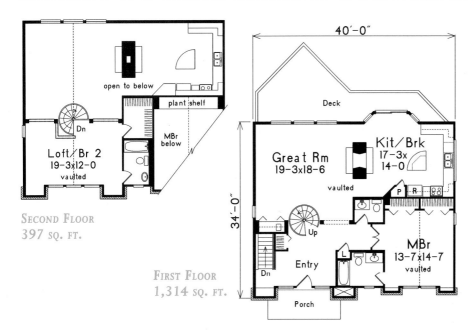

SECOND FLOOR
397 SQ. FT.

FIRST FLOOR
1,314 SQ. FT.

Ideal Home For Lake, Mountains Or Seaside

SPECIAL FEATURES

- 1,711 total square feet of living area

- Colossal entry leads to a vaulted great room with exposed beams, two-story window wall, brick fireplace, wet bar and balcony

- Bayed breakfast room shares the fireplace and joins a sun-drenched kitchen and sundeck

- Vaulted first floor master suite with double entry doors, closets and bookshelves

- Spiral stair and balcony dramatizes a loft that doubles as a spacious second bedroom

- 2 bedrooms, 2 1/2 baths

- Basement foundation

REAR VIEW

Stylish Retreat
For A Narrow Lot

SPECIAL FEATURES

- 1,084 total square feet of living area

- Delightful country porch for quiet evenings

- The living room offers a front feature window which invites the sun and includes a fireplace and dining area with private patio

- The U-shaped kitchen features lots of cabinets and bayed breakfast room with built-in pantry

- Both bedrooms have walk-in closets and access to their own bath

- 2 bedrooms, 2 baths

- Basement foundation

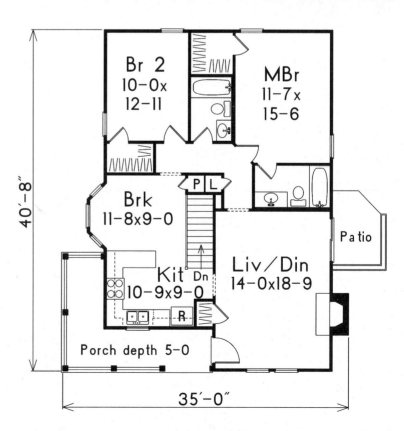

Year-Round Hideaway

SPECIAL FEATURES

- 416 total square feet of living area
- Open floor plan creates spacious feeling
- Covered porch has rustic appeal
- Plenty of cabinetry and workspace in kitchen
- Large linen closet centrally located and close to bath
- Sleeping area, 1 bath
- Slab foundation

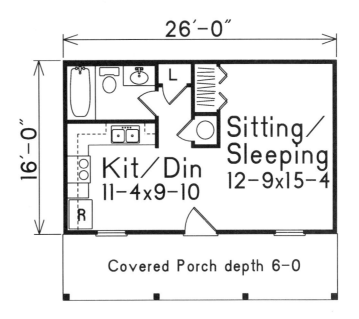

26'-0"

16'-0"

Sitting/ Sleeping 12-9x15-4

Kit/Din 11-4x9-10

L

R

Covered Porch depth 6-0

Four Bedroom Living For A Narrow Lot

SPECIAL FEATURES

- 1,452 total square feet of living area

- Large living room features cozy corner fireplace, bayed dining area and access from entry with guest closet

- Forward master bedroom suite enjoys having its own bath and linen closet

- Three additional bedrooms share a bath with double-bowl vanity

- 4 bedrooms, 2 baths

- Basement foundation

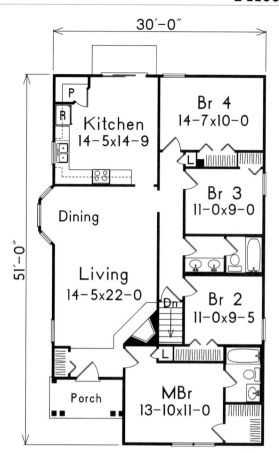

Rustic Haven

SPECIAL FEATURES

- 1,275 total square feet of living area
- Wall shingles and stone veneer fireplace all fashion an irresistible rustic appeal
- Living area features fireplace and opens to an efficient kitchen
- Two bedrooms on second floor
- 4 bedrooms, 2 baths
- Basement foundation, drawings also include crawl space and slab foundations

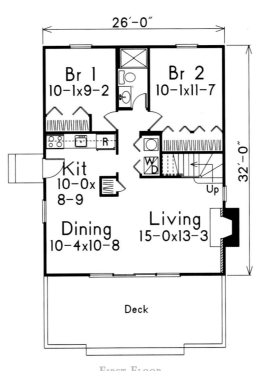

FIRST FLOOR
832 SQ. FT.

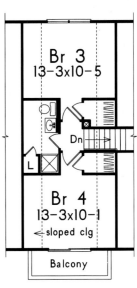

SECOND FLOOR
443 SQ. FT.

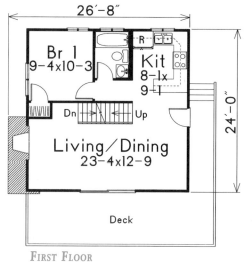

26'-8"

24'-0"

Br 1
9-4x10-3

Kit
8-1x
9-1

R

Dn   Up

Living/Dining
23-4x12-9

Deck

FIRST FLOOR
576 SQ. FT.

Dorm
8-8x13-7

Dorm
8-8x13-7

sloped
clg

sloped
clg

Dn

Br 2
11-6x9-5

Br 3
11-6x9-5

Balcony

SECOND FLOOR
528 SQ. FT.

LOWER LEVEL
576 SQ. FT.

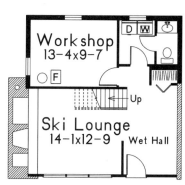

Workshop
13-4x9-7

D   W

F

Up

Ski Lounge
14-1x12-9

Wet Hall

Ski Chalet With Style

SPECIAL FEATURES

- 1,680 total square feet of living area
- Highly functional lower level includes wet hall with storage, laundry area, work shop and cozy ski lounge with enormous fireplace
- First floor warmed by large fireplace in living/dining area which features spacious wrap-around deck
- Lots of sleeping space for guests or a large family
- 5 bedrooms, 2 1/2 baths
- Basement foundation

To order blueprints use the form on page 114 or call 1-800-DREAM HOME (373-2646)

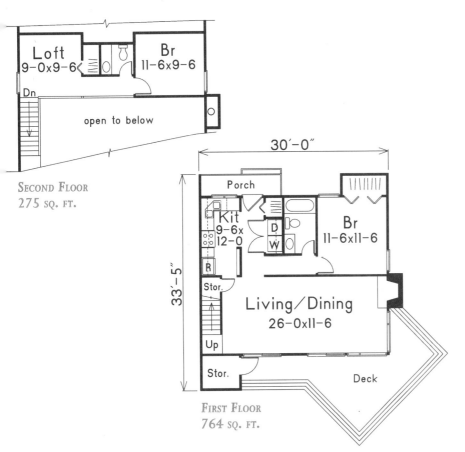

Loft
9-0x9-6

Br
11-6x9-6

Dn

open to below

SECOND FLOOR
275 SQ. FT.

30'-0"

Porch

Kit
9-6x
12-0

Br
11-6x11-6

33'-5"

Stor.

Living/Dining
26-0x11-6

Up

Stor.

Deck

FIRST FLOOR
764 SQ. FT.

A Vacation Home For All Seasons

SPECIAL FEATURES

- 1,039 total square feet of living area
- Cathedral construction provides the maximum in living area openness
- Expansive glass viewing walls
- Two decks, front and back
- Charming second story loft arrangement
- Simple, low-maintenance construction
- 2 bedrooms, 1 1/2 baths
- Crawl space foundation

Cozy Front Porch
Welcomes Guests

SPECIAL FEATURES

- 1,393 total square feet of living area
- L-shaped kitchen features walk-in pantry, island cooktop and is convenient to laundry room and dining area
- Master bedroom features large walk-in closet and private bath with separate tub and shower
- Convenient storage/coat closet in hall
- View to the patio from the dining area
- 3 bedrooms, 2 baths, 2-car detached garage
- Crawl space foundation, drawings also include slab foundation

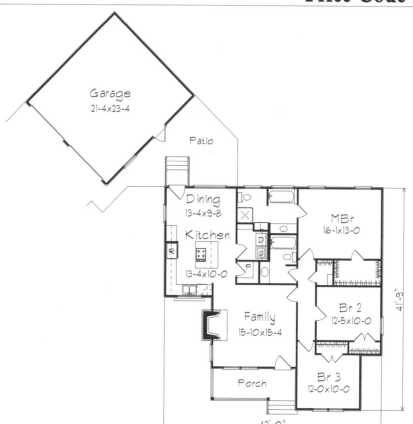

Plan #X22-0273

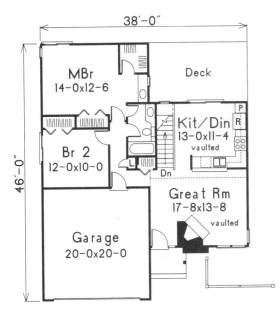

Compact Ranch An Ideal Starter Home

SPECIAL FEATURES

- 988 total square feet of living area
- Great room features corner fireplace
- Vaulted ceiling and corner windows add space and light in great room
- Eat-in kitchen with vaulted ceiling accesses deck for outdoor living
- Master bedroom features separate vanity and private access to the bath
- 2 bedrooms, 1 bath, 2-car garage
- Basement foundation

Plan #X22-0766

Price Code AA

Vaulted Ceiling Adds Spaciousness

SPECIAL FEATURES

- 990 total square feet of living area
- Wrap-around porch on two sides of this home
- Private and efficiently designed
- Space for efficiency washer and dryer unit for convenience
- 2 bedrooms, 1 bath
- Crawl space foundation

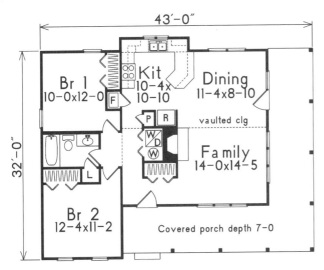

To order blueprints use the form on page 114 or call 1-800-DREAM HOME (373-2646)

Year-Round Or Weekend Getaway Home

SPECIAL FEATURES

- 1,339 total square feet of living area
- Full-length covered porch enhances front facade
- Vaulted ceiling and stone fireplace add drama to family room
- Walk-in closets in bedrooms provide ample storage space
- Combined kitchen/dining area adjoins family room for perfect entertaining space
- 3 bedrooms, 2 1/2 baths
- Crawl space foundation

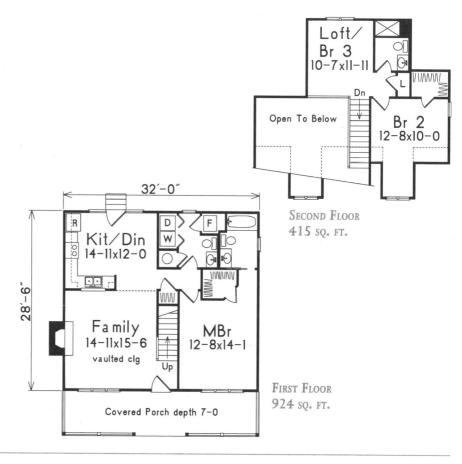

SECOND FLOOR
415 SQ. FT.

FIRST FLOOR
924 SQ. FT.

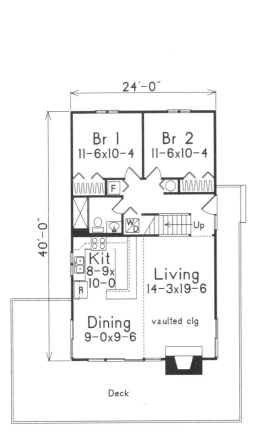

24'-0"

40'-0"

Br 1
11-6x10-4

Br 2
11-6x10-4

F

W
D

Up

Kit
8-9x
10-0

R

Living
14-3x19-6

vaulted clg

Dining
9-0x9-6

Deck

FIRST FLOOR
960 SQ. FT.

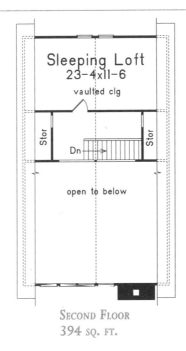

Sleeping Loft
23-4x11-6

vaulted clg

Stor

Dn

Stor

open to below

SECOND FLOOR
394 SQ. FT.

Leisure Living With Interior Surprise

SPECIAL FEATURES

- 1,354 total square feet of living area

- Soaring ceilings highlight the kitchen, living and dining areas creating dramatic excitement

- A spectacular large deck surrounds the front and both sides of home

- An impressive kitchen is U-shaped with wrap-around breakfast bar and shares fantastic views with both upper and lower areas through an awesome wall of glass

- Two bedrooms with a bath, a loft for sleeping and second floor balcony overlooking living area, complete the home

- 3 bedrooms, 1 bath

- Crawl space foundation

Plan #X22-1293

Perfect Home For Escaping To The Outdoors

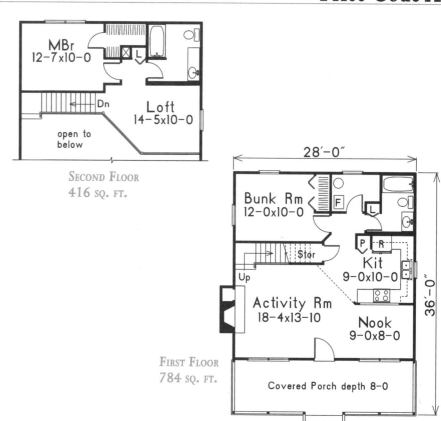

SECOND FLOOR
416 SQ. FT.

MBr 12-7x10-0

Loft 14-5x10-0

open to below

Dn

FIRST FLOOR
784 SQ. FT.

28'-0"

36'-0"

Bunk Rm 12-0x10-0

Kit 9-0x10-0

Activity Rm 18-4x13-10

Nook 9-0x8-0

Stor

Up

Covered Porch depth 8-0

SPECIAL FEATURES

- 1,200 total square feet of living area
- Enjoy lazy summer evenings on this magnificent porch
- Activity area has fireplace and ascending stair from cozy loft
- Kitchen features built-in pantry
- Master suite enjoys large bath, walk-in closet and cozy loft overlooking room below
- 2 bedrooms, 2 baths
- Crawl space foundation

A Special Home For Views

SPECIAL FEATURES

- 1,684 total square feet of living area

- Delightful wrap-around porch anchored by full masonry fireplace

- The vaulted great room includes a large bay window, fireplace, dining balcony and atrium window wall

- His and hers walk-in closets, large luxury bath and sliding doors to exterior balcony are a few fantastic features of the master bedroom

- 3 bedrooms, 2 baths, 2-car drive under garage

- Walk-out basement foundation

- Atrium open to 611 square feet of optional living area on the lower level

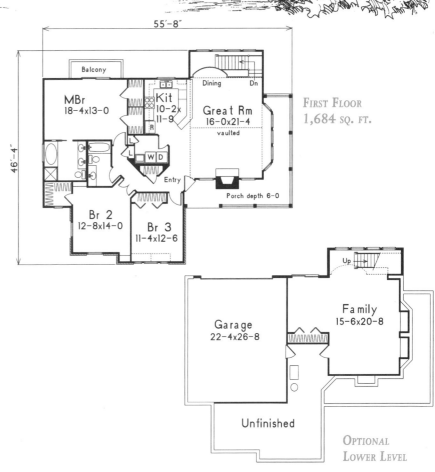

55'-8"

46'-4"

Balcony

MBr
18-4x13-0

Kit
10-2x
11-9

Dining   Dn

Great Rm
16-0x21-4
vaulted

R

L W D

Entry

Porch depth 6-0

Br 2
12-8x14-0

Br 3
11-4x12-6

FIRST FLOOR
1,684 SQ. FT.

Up

Garage
22-4x26-8

Family
15-6x20-8

Unfinished

OPTIONAL
LOWER LEVEL

Plan #X22-0670

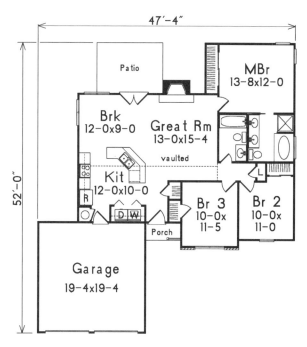

Brick And Siding Enhance This Home

SPECIAL FEATURES

- 1,170 total square feet of living area
- Master bedroom enjoys privacy at the rear of this home
- Kitchen has angled bar that overlooks great room and breakfast area
- Living areas combine to create a greater sense of spaciousness
- Great room has a cozy fireplace
- 3 bedrooms, 2 baths, 2-car garage
- Slab foundation
- Basement foundation

Plan #X22-0547

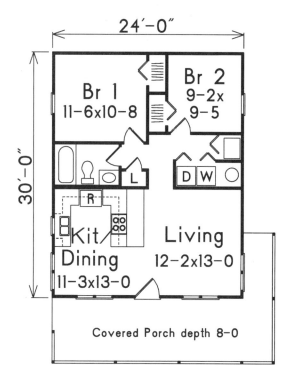

Designed For Comfort And Utility

SPECIAL FEATURES

- 720 total square feet of living area
- Abundant windows in living and dining rooms provide generous sunlight
- Secluded laundry area with handy storage closet
- U-shaped kitchen has large breakfast bar which opens into living area
- Large covered deck offers plenty of outdoor living space
- 2 bedrooms, 1 bath
- Crawl space foundation, drawings also include slab foundation

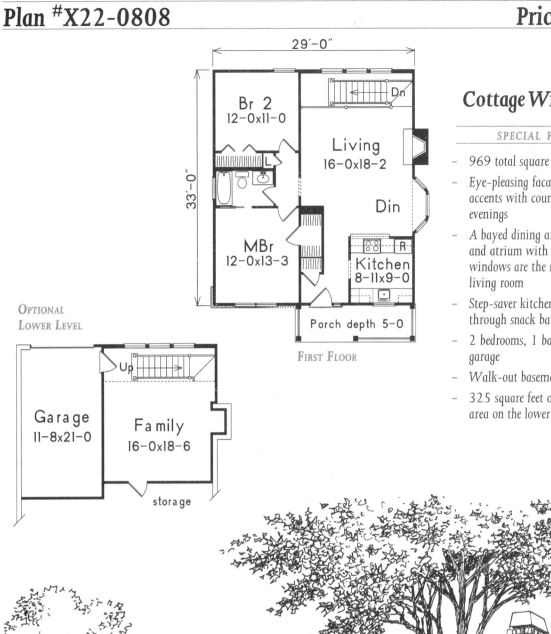

29'-0"

Br 2
12-0x11-0

Living
16-0x18-2

33'-0"

Dn

Din

MBr
12-0x13-3

Kitchen
8-11x9-0

R

L

Porch depth 5-0

FIRST FLOOR

OPTIONAL
LOWER LEVEL

Up

Garage
11-8x21-0

Family
16-0x18-6

storage

Cottage With Atrium

SPECIAL FEATURES

- 969 total square feet of living area

- Eye-pleasing facade enjoys stone accents with country porch for quiet evenings

- A bayed dining area, cozy fireplace and atrium with sunny two-story windows are the many features of the living room

- Step-saver kitchen includes a pass-through snack bar

- 2 bedrooms, 1 bath, 1-car rear entry garage

- Walk-out basement foundation

- 325 square feet of optional living area on the lower level

Surrounding Porch
For Country Views

SPECIAL FEATURES

- 1,428 total square feet of living area

- Large vaulted family room opens to dining and kitchen area with breakfast bar and access to surrounding porch

- First floor master suite offers large bath, walk-in closet and nearby laundry facilities

- A spacious loft/bedroom #3 overlooking family room and an additional bedroom and bath conclude the second floor

- 3 bedrooms, 2 baths

- Basement foundation

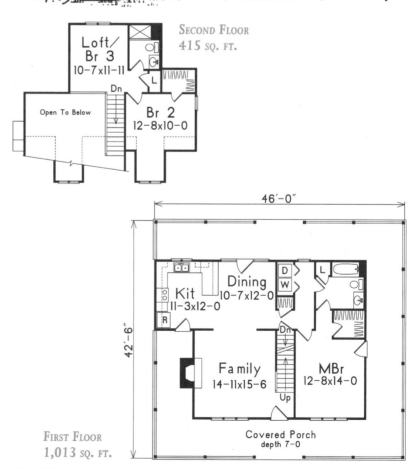

SECOND FLOOR
415 SQ. FT.

Loft/
Br 3
10-7x11-11

Open To Below

Dn

L

Br 2
12-8x10-0

FIRST FLOOR
1,013 SQ. FT.

46'-0"

42'-6"

Kit
11-3x12-0

Dining
10-7x12-0

D
W

L

Family
14-11x15-6

Dn

MBr
12-8x14-0

Up

Covered Porch
depth 7-0

To order blueprints use the form on page 114 or call 1-800-DREAM HOME (373-2646)

Dramatic Expanse Of Windows

SPECIAL FEATURES

- 1,660 total square feet of living area
- Convenient gear and equipment room
- Spacious living and dining rooms look even larger with the openness of the foyer and kitchen
- Large wrap-around deck, a great plus for outdoor living
- Broad balcony overlooks living and dining rooms
- 3 bedrooms, 3 baths
- Partial basement/crawl space foundation, drawings also include slab foundation

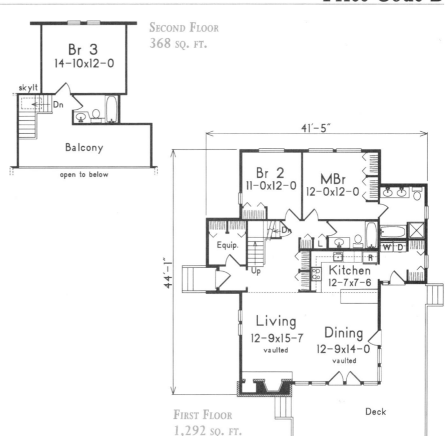

SECOND FLOOR
368 SQ. FT.

Br 3
14-10x12-0

skylt

Dn

Balcony

open to below

41'-5"

44'-1"

Br 2
11-0x12-0

MBr
12-0x12-0

Equip.

Up

Kitchen
12-7x7-6

Living
12-9x15-7
vaulted

Dining
12-9x14-0
vaulted

Deck

FIRST FLOOR
1,292 SQ. FT.

Recessed Stone Entry Provides A Unique Accent

SPECIAL FEATURES

- 717 total square feet of living area
- Incline ladder leads up to cozy loft area
- Living room features plenty of windows and vaulted ceiling
- U-shaped kitchen includes a small bay window at the sink
- 1 bedroom, 1 bath
- Slab foundation

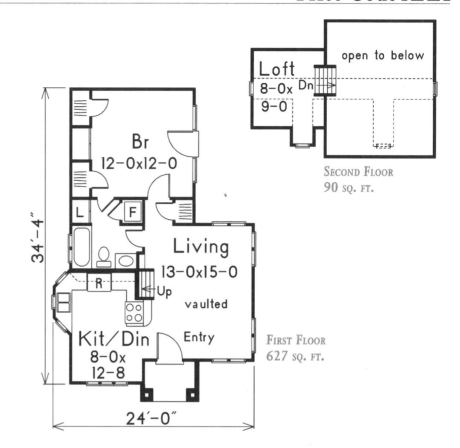

Second Floor
90 SQ. FT.

First Floor
627 SQ. FT.

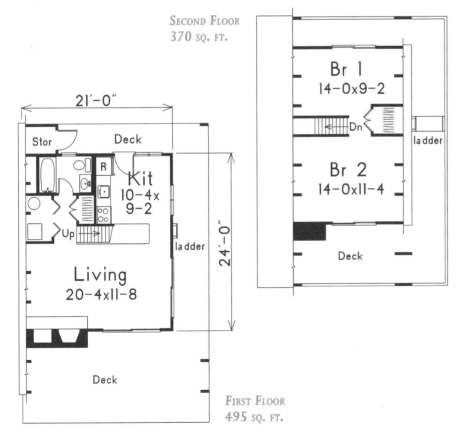

SECOND FLOOR
370 SQ. FT.

Br 1
14-0x9-2

Dn

ladder

Br 2
14-0x11-4

Deck

21'-0"

Stor

Deck

Kit
10-4x
9-2

R

24'-0"

Up

ladder

Living
20-4x11-8

Deck

FIRST FLOOR
495 SQ. FT.

Terrific Design
Loaded With Extras

SPECIAL FEATURES

- 865 total square feet of living area

- Central living area provides an enormous amount of space for gathering around the fireplace

- Outdoor ladder on wrap-around deck connects top deck with main deck

- Kitchen is bright and cheerful with lots of windows and access to deck

- 2 bedrooms, 1 bath

- Pier foundation

Plan #X22-0696

Small And Cozy Cabin

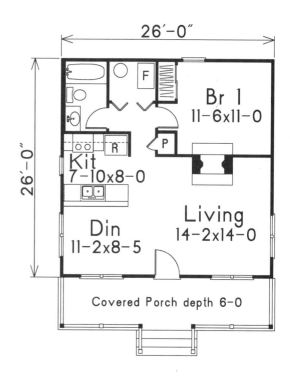

26'-0"

26'-0"

Br 1
11-6x11-0

Kit
7-10x8-0

Din
11-2x8-5

Living
14-2x14-0

F

R

P

Covered Porch depth 6-0

SPECIAL FEATURES

- 676 total square feet of living area
- See-through fireplace between bedroom and living area adds character
- Combined dining and living areas create an open feeling
- Full-length front covered porch perfect for enjoying the outdoors
- Additional storage available in utility room
- 1 bedroom, 1 bath
- Crawl space foundation

Plan #X22-N145

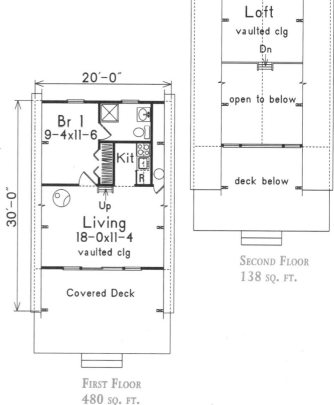

An A-Frame For Every Environment

20'-0"

30'-0"

Br 1
9-4x11-6

Kit

Up

Living
18-0x11-4
vaulted clg

Covered Deck

FIRST FLOOR
480 SQ. FT.

Loft
vaulted clg

Dn

open to below

deck below

SECOND FLOOR
138 SQ. FT.

SPECIAL FEATURES

- 618 total square feet of living area
- Memorable family events are certain to be enjoyed on this fabulous partially covered sundeck
- Equally impressive is the living area with its cathedral ceiling and exposed rafters
- A kitchenette, bedroom and bath conclude the first floor with a delightful sleeping loft above bedroom and bath
- 1 bedroom, 1 bath
- Pier foundation

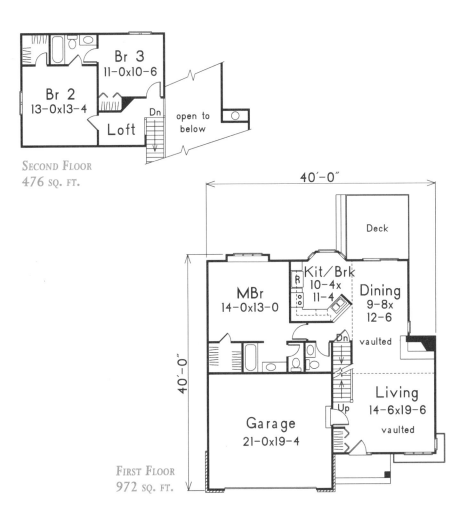

SECOND FLOOR
476 SQ. FT.

Br 2
13-0x13-4

Br 3
11-0x10-6

Loft

Dn

open to below

40'-0"

40'-0"

Deck

MBr
14-0x13-0

Kit/Brk
10-4x
11-4

Dining
9-8x
12-6

vaulted

Dn

Living
14-6x19-6

vaulted

Up

Garage
21-0x19-4

FIRST FLOOR
972 SQ. FT.

Vaulted Living Area
With Corner Fireplace

SPECIAL FEATURES

- 1,448 total square feet of living area
- Dining room conveniently adjoins kitchen and accesses rear deck
- Private first floor master bedroom
- Secondary bedrooms share a bath and cozy loft area
- 3 bedrooms, 2 1/2 baths, 2-car garage
- Basement foundation

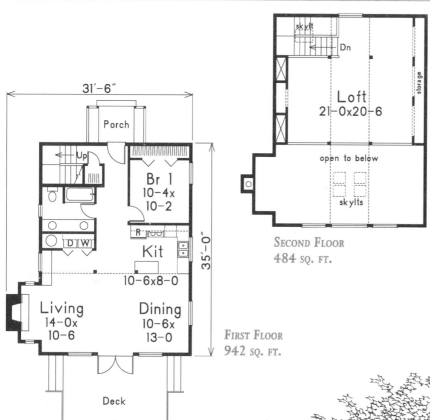

31'-6"

Porch

Up

Br 1
10-4x
10-2

Kit
10-6x8-0

Living
14-0x
10-6

Dining
10-6x
13-0

35'-0"

FIRST FLOOR
942 SQ. FT.

Deck

skylt

Dn

Loft
21-0x20-6

storage

open to below

skylts

SECOND FLOOR
484 SQ. FT.

Large Loft Area Offers Endless Possibilities

SPECIAL FEATURES

- 1,426 total square feet of living area

- Large front deck invites outdoor relaxation

- Expansive windows, skylights, vaulted ceiling and fireplace enhance the living/dining combination

- Nook, adjacent to the living room, has a cozy window seat

- Kitchen becomes a part of the living/ dining area

- 1 bedroom, 1 bath

- Crawl space foundation

To order blueprints use the form on page 114 or call 1-800-DREAM HOME (373-2646)

Ornate Corner Porch Catches The Eye

SPECIAL FEATURES

- 1,550 total square feet of living area

- Impressive front entrance with a wrap-around covered porch and raised foyer

- Corner fireplace provides a focal point in the vaulted great room

- Loft is easily converted to a third bedroom or activity center

- Large family/kitchen area includes greenhouse windows and access to the deck and utility area

- Secondary bedroom has a large dormer and window seat

- 2 bedrooms, 2 1/2 baths, 2-car garage

- Basement foundation

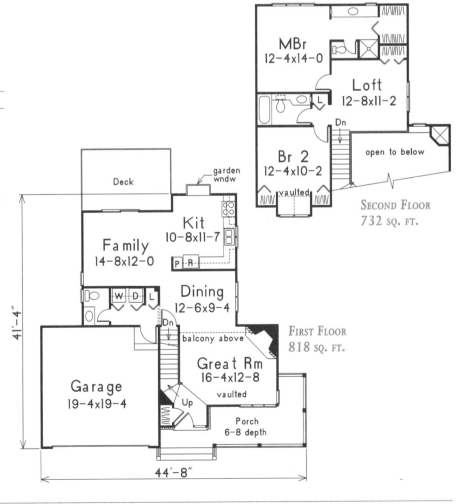

MBr
12-4x14-0

Loft
12-8x11-2

Br 2
12-4x10-2

open to below

vaulted

SECOND FLOOR
732 SQ. FT.

Deck

garden wndw

Kit
10-8x11-7

Family
14-8x12-0

P R

W D L

Dining
12-6x9-4

Dn

balcony above

FIRST FLOOR
818 SQ. FT.

Garage
19-4x19-4

Up

Great Rm
16-4x12-8
vaulted

Porch
6-8 depth

41'-4"

44'-8"

Contemporary Escape

SPECIAL FEATURES

- 1,836 total square feet of living area

- Foyer sparkles with spiral stair, sloped ceilings and celestial windows

- Living room enjoys fireplace with bookshelves and views to outdoors

- U-shaped kitchen includes eat-in breakfast area and dining nearby

- Master suite revels in having a balcony overlooking the living room, a large walk-in closet and private bath

- 3 bedrooms, 2 1/2 baths

- Crawl space foundation, drawings also include slab foundation

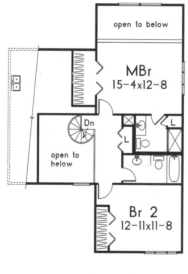

SECOND FLOOR
748 SQ. FT.

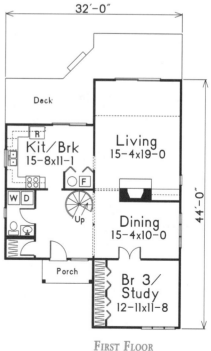

FIRST FLOOR
1,088 SQ. FT.

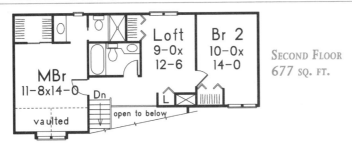

SECOND FLOOR
677 SQ. FT.

Loft
9-0x
12-6

Br 2
10-0x
14-0

MBr
11-8x14-0

Dn

vaulted

open to below

L

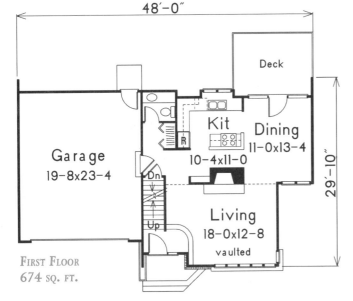

48'-0"

29'-10"

Deck

Kit
10-4x11-0

Dining
11-0x13-4

Garage
19-8x23-4

Dn

Up

R

Living
18-0x12-8
vaulted

FIRST FLOOR
674 SQ. FT.

Tall Windows, Sweeping Roof Lines Make A Sizable Impression

SPECIAL FEATURES

- 1,351 total square feet of living area
- Roof lines and vaulted ceilings make this home appear larger than its true size
- Central fireplace provides a focal point for dining and living areas
- Master bedroom suite is highlighted by a roomy window seat and a walk-in closet
- 3 bedrooms, 2 1/2 baths, 2-car garage
- Basement foundation

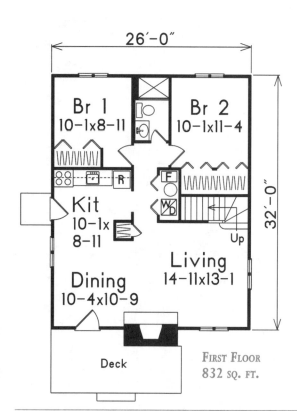

26'-0"

32'-0"

Br 1
10-1x8-11

Br 2
10-1x11-4

Kit
10-1x
8-11

Up

Living
14-11x13-1

Dining
10-4x10-9

Deck

First Floor
832 SQ. FT.

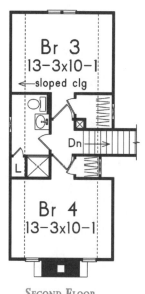

Br 3
13-3x10-1
←sloped clg

Dn

L

Br 4
13-3x10-1

Second Floor
448 SQ. FT.

Cozy Cottage Living

SPECIAL FEATURES

- 1,332 total square feet of living area

- A front porch deck, ornate porch roof, massive stone fireplace and old English windows all generate inviting appeal

- Large living room accesses kitchen with spacious dining area

- Two spacious bedrooms with ample closet space comprise second floor

- 4 bedrooms, 2 baths

- Basement foundation, drawings also include slab and crawl space foundations

Plan #X22-0658

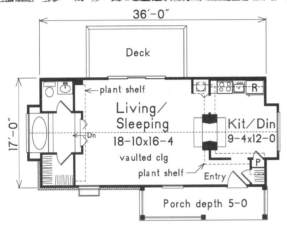

Sensational Cottage Retreat

SPECIAL FEATURES

- 647 total square feet of living area
- Large vaulted room for living/ sleeping with plant shelves on each end, stone fireplace and wide glass doors for views
- Roomy kitchen is vaulted and has a bayed dining area and fireplace
- Step down into a sunken and vaulted bath featuring a 6'-0" whirlpool tub-in-a-bay with shelves at each end for storage
- A large palladian window adorns each end of the cottage giving a cheery atmosphere throughout
- 1 living/sleeping room, 1 bath
- Crawl space foundation

Plan #X22-N114

Price Code AAA

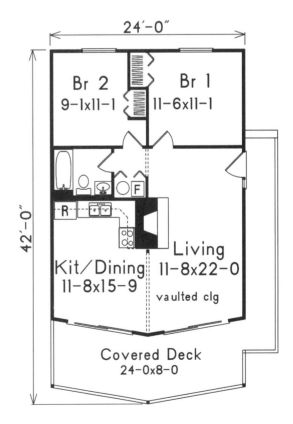

Riverside Views From Covered Deck

SPECIAL FEATURES

- 792 total square feet of living area
- Attractive exterior features wood posts and beams, wrap-around deck with railing and glass sliding doors with transoms
- Living, dining and kitchen areas enjoy sloped ceilings, cozy fireplace and views over deck
- Two bedrooms share a bath just off the hall
- 2 bedrooms, 1 bath
- Crawl space foundation, drawings also include slab foundation

Perfect Vacation Home

SPECIAL FEATURES

- 1,230 total square feet of living area

- Spacious living room accesses huge sun deck

- One of the second floor bedrooms features a balcony overlooking the deck

- Kitchen with dining area accesses outdoors

- Washer and dryer tucked under stairs

- 3 bedrooms, 1 bath

- Crawl space foundation, drawings also include slab foundation

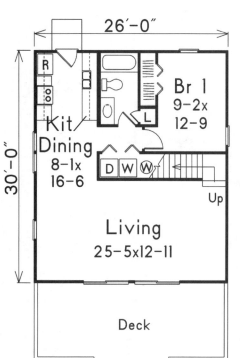

26'-0"

30'-0"

R

Kit
Dining
8-1x
16-6

Br 1
9-2x
12-9

D W W

Up

Living
25-5x12-11

Deck

FIRST FLOOR
780 SQ. FT.

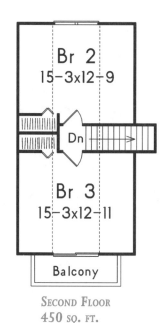

Br 2
15-3x12-9

Dn

Br 3
15-3x12-11

Balcony

SECOND FLOOR
450 SQ. FT.

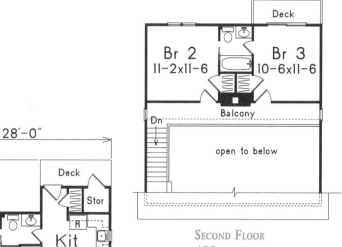

Second Floor
488 SQ. FT.

First Floor
811 SQ. FT.

28'-0"

46'-0"

Deck

Stor

R

Br 1
9-11x11-6

Kit
10-7x
8-3

D
W

Din
10-10x
7-3

Living
23-10x12-3

Up

Deck

Deck

Br 2
11-2x11-6

Br 3
10-6x11-6

Balcony

open to below

Dn

Breathtaking Balcony Overlook

SPECIAL FEATURES

- 1,299 total square feet of living area

- Convenient storage for skis, etc. located outside front entrance

- Kitchen and dining room receive light from box bay window

- Large vaulted living room features cozy fireplace and overlook from second floor balcony

- Two second floor bedrooms share jack and jill bath

- Second floor balcony extends over entire length of living room below

- 3 bedrooms, 2 baths

- Crawl space foundation, drawings also include slab foundation

Country Retreat For Quiet Times

SPECIAL FEATURES

- 1,211 total square feet of living area

- Extraordinary views are enjoyed from vaulted family room through sliding doors

- Functional kitchen features snack bar and laundry closet

- Bedroom and bunk room complete first floor while a large bedroom with two storage areas and balcony overlook, complete the second floor

- Plan includes third bedroom option which creates an additional 223 square feet of living area

- 3 bedrooms, 1 bath

- Crawl space foundation, drawings also include basement foundation

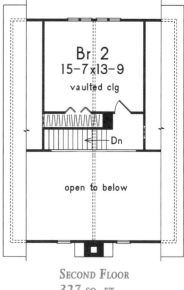

Br 2
15-7x13-9
vaulted clg

Dn

open to below

SECOND FLOOR
327 SQ. FT.

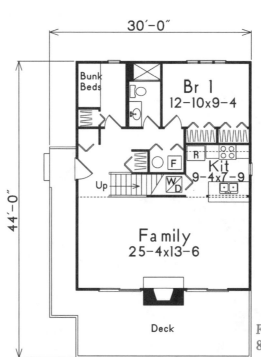

30'-0"

44'-0"

Bunk Beds

Br 1
12-10x9-4

R

Kit
9-4x7-9

F

W D

Up

Family
25-4x13-6

Deck

FIRST FLOOR
884 SQ. FT.

Plan #X22-0502

Price Code AAA

Perfect Home For *A Small Family*

SPECIAL FEATURES

- 864 total square feet of living area
- L-shaped kitchen with convenient pantry is adjacent to dining area
- Easy access to laundry area, linen closet and storage closet
- Both bedrooms include ample closet space
- 2 bedrooms, 1 bath
- Crawl space foundation, drawings also include basement and slab foundations

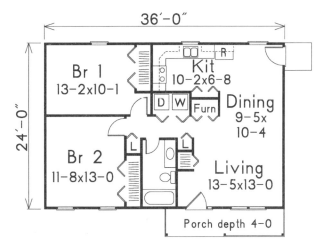

Plan #X22-0769

Price Code A

Flexible Design Is Popular

SPECIAL FEATURES

- 1,440 total square feet of living area
- Open floor plan with access to covered porches in front and back
- Lots of linen, pantry and closet space throughout
- Laundry/mud room between kitchen and garage is a convenient feature
- 2 bedrooms, 2 baths
- Basement foundation

Plan #X22-N131

Covered Porch Adds To Perfect Outdoor Getaway

SPECIAL FEATURES

- 733 total square feet of living area
- Bedrooms separate from kitchen and living area for privacy
- Lots of closet space throughout this home
- Centrally located bath is easily accessible
- Kitchen features door to rear of home and a door separating it from the rest of the home
- 2 bedrooms, 1 bath
- Pier foundation

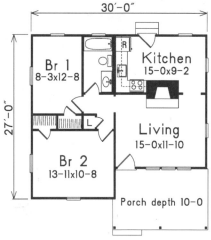

30'-0"

27'-0"

Br 1
8-3x12-8

Kitchen
15-0x9-2

Living
15-0x11-10

Br 2
13-11x10-8

Porch depth 10-0

Plan #X22-0765

Price Code AA

Rustic Design With Modern Features

SPECIAL FEATURES

- 1,000 total square feet of living area
- Large mud room with separate covered porch entrance
- Full-length covered front porch
- Bedrooms on opposite sides of the home for privacy
- Vaulted ceiling creates an open and spacious feeling
- 2 bedrooms, 1 bath
- Crawl space foundation

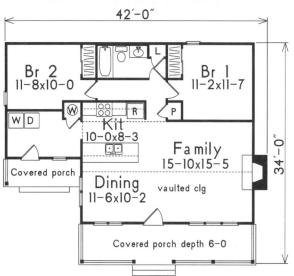

42'-0"

34'-0"

Br 2
11-8x10-0

Br 1
11-2x11-7

W D

Kit
10-0x8-3

Family
15-10x15-5

Covered porch

Dining
11-6x10-2

vaulted clg

Covered porch depth 6-0

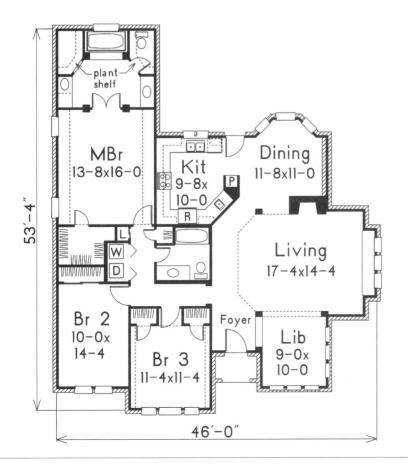

plant shelf

MBr
13-8x16-0

Kit
9-8x
10-0

Dining
11-8x11-0

P

L
W
D
R

Living
17-4x14-4

Br 2
10-0x
14-4

Br 3
11-4x11-4

Foyer

Lib
9-0x
10-0

53'-4"

46'-0"

Corner Windows
Grace Library

SPECIAL FEATURES

- 1,824 total square feet of living area

- Living room features 10' ceiling, fireplace and media center

- Dining room includes bay window and convenient kitchen access

- Master bedroom features large walk-in closet and double-doors leading into master bath

- Modified U-shaped kitchen features pantry and bar

- 3 bedrooms, 2 baths, 2-car detached garage

- Slab foundation

Dramatic Look For Quiet Hideaway

SPECIAL FEATURES

- 1,750 total square feet of living area
- Family room brightened by floor-to-ceiling windows and sliding doors providing access to large deck
- Second floor sitting area perfect for game room or entertaining
- Kitchen includes eat-in dining area plus outdoor dining patio as a bonus
- Plenty of closet and storage space throughout
- 3 bedrooms, 2 baths
- Basement foundation, drawings also include crawl space and slab foundations

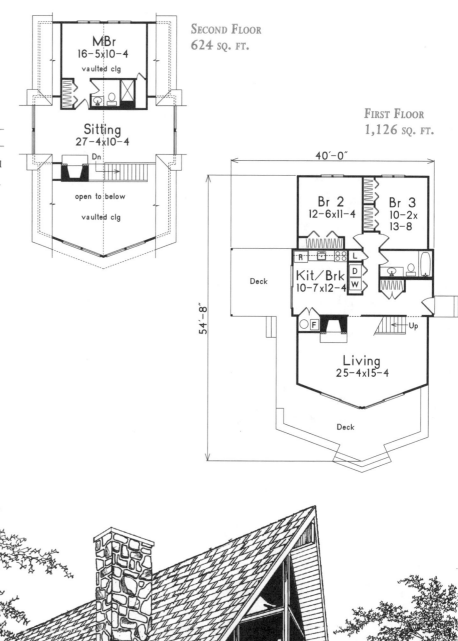

SECOND FLOOR
624 SQ. FT.

FIRST FLOOR
1,126 SQ. FT.

To order blueprints use the form on page 114 or call 1-800-DREAM HOME **(373-2646)**

Exciting Living For A Narrow Sloping Lot

SPECIAL FEATURES

- 1,200 total square feet of living area
- Entry leads to a large dining area which opens to kitchen and sun drenched living room
- An expansive window wall in the two-story atrium lends space and light to living room with fireplace
- The large kitchen features a breakfast bar, built-in pantry and storage galore
- 2 bedrooms, 1 bath
- Walk-out basement foundation
- Optional lower level has an additional 697 square feet of living area and includes a family room, bedroom #3 and a bath

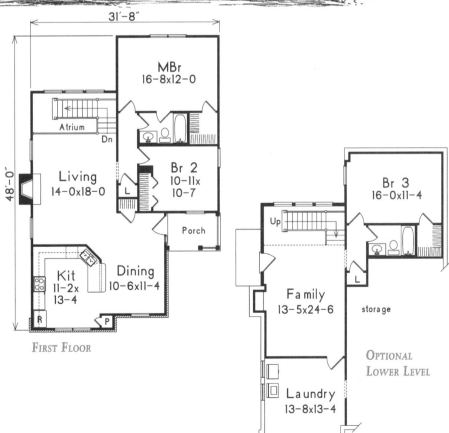

31'-8"

48'-0"

MBr
16-8x12-0

Atrium

Dn

Living
14-0x18-0

Br 2
10-11x
10-7

L

Porch

Kit
11-2x
13-4

Dining
10-6x11-4

R

P

FIRST FLOOR

Br 3
16-0x11-4

Up

L

Family
13-5x24-6

storage

Laundry
13-8x13-4

OPTIONAL
LOWER LEVEL

Dormer And Covered Porch Add To Country Charm

SPECIAL FEATURES

- 954 total square feet of living area
- Kitchen has cozy bayed eating area
- Master bedroom has a walk-in closet and private bath
- Large great room has access to the back porch
- Convenient coat closet near front entry
- 3 bedrooms, 2 baths
- Basement foundation

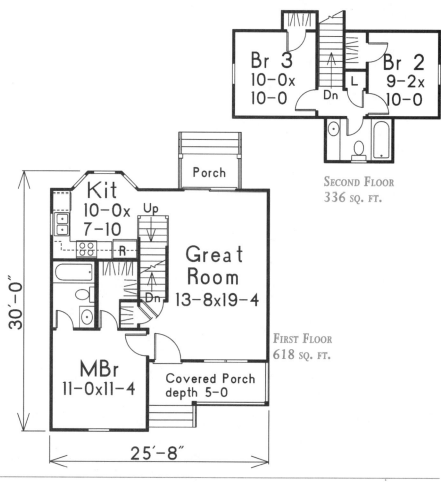

Br 3 10-0x 10-0

Br 2 9-2x 10-0

Dn L

SECOND FLOOR
336 SQ. FT.

Kit 10-0x 7-10

Porch

Up

Great Room 13-8x19-4

Dn

R

30'-0"

MBr 11-0x11-4

Covered Porch depth 5-0

FIRST FLOOR
618 SQ. FT.

25'-8"

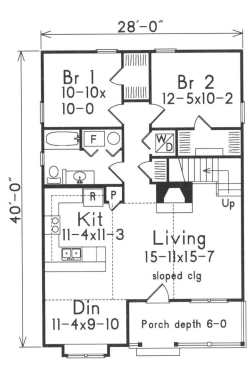

28'-0"

40'-0"

Br 1
10-10x
10-0

Br 2
12-5x10-2

F

W/D

R P

Kit
11-4x11-3

Up

Living
15-11x15-7
sloped clg

Din
11-4x9-10

Porch depth 6-0

FIRST FLOOR
1,032 SQ. FT.

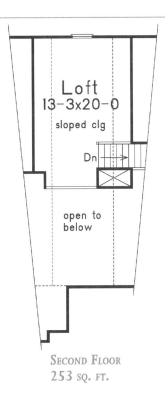

Loft
13-3x20-0
sloped clg

Dn

open to
below

SECOND FLOOR
253 SQ. FT.

Cozy And Functional Design

SPECIAL FEATURES

- 1,285 total square feet of living area
- Dining nook creates warm feeling with sunny box bay window
- Second floor loft perfect for recreation space or office hideaway
- Bedrooms include walk-in closets allowing extra storage space
- Kitchen, dining and living areas combine making perfect gathering place
- 2 bedrooms, 1 bath
- Crawl space foundation

Large Windows Brighten Home Inside And Out

SPECIAL FEATURES

- 1,260 total square feet of living area
- Living area features enormous stone fireplace and sliding glass doors for accessing deck
- Kitchen/dining area is organized with lots of cabinet and counter space
- Second bedroom is vaulted and has closet space along one entire wall
- 3 bedrooms, 1 bath
- Crawl space foundation

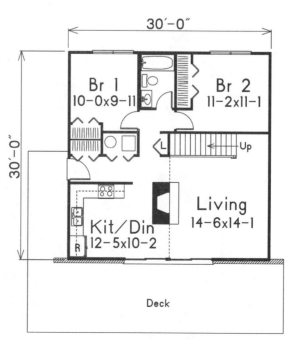

30'-0"

30'-0"

Br 1
10-0x9-11

Br 2
11-2x11-1

Kit/Din
12-5x10-2

Living
14-6x14-1

Up

Deck

Br 3
12-2x11-1
vaulted clg

Dn

Loft

open to below

SECOND FLOOR
360 SQ. FT.

FIRST FLOOR
900 SQ. FT.

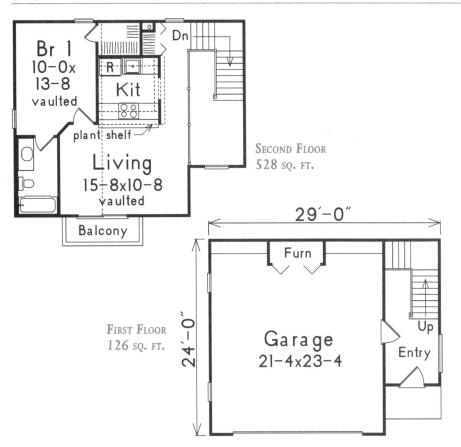

Br 1
10-0x
13-8
vaulted

Kit

Dn

R

plant shelf

Living
15-8x10-8
vaulted

Balcony

SECOND FLOOR
528 SQ. FT.

29'-0"

24'-0"

FIRST FLOOR
126 SQ. FT.

Furn

Garage
21-4x23-4

Up

Entry

Apartment Garage With Imagination

SPECIAL FEATURES

- 654 total square feet of living area
- Two-story vaulted entry has a balcony overlook and large windows to welcome the sun
- Vaulted living room is open to a pass-through kitchen and breakfast bar with an overhead plant shelf and features sliding glass doors to an outdoor balcony
- The bedroom with vaulted ceiling offers private bath and walk-in closet
- 1 bedroom, 1 bath, 2-car garage
- Slab foundation

Plan #X22-0274

Breakfast Bay Area Opens To Deck

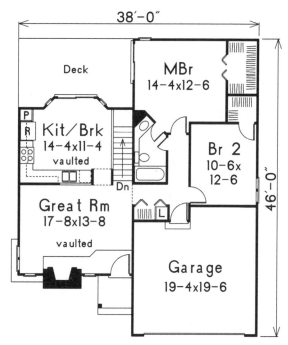

SPECIAL FEATURES

- 1,020 total square feet of living area
- Kitchen features open stairs, pass-through to great room, pantry and deck access
- Master bedroom features private entrance to bath, large walk-in closet and sliding doors to deck
- Informal entrance into home through the garage
- Great room with vaulted ceiling and fireplace
- 2 bedrooms, 1 bath, 2-car garage
- Basement foundation

Plan #X22-0650

Price Code AA

Quaint Cottage With Inviting Front Porch

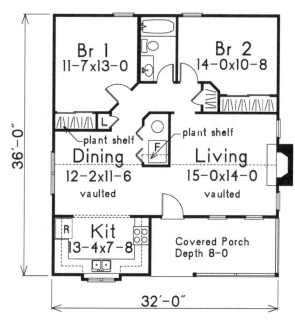

SPECIAL FEATURES

- 1,020 total square feet of living area
- Living room is warmed by a fireplace
- Dining and living rooms are enhanced by vaulted ceilings and plant shelves
- U-shaped kitchen with large window over the sink
- 2 bedrooms, 1 bath
- Slab foundation

Innovative Ranch Has Cozy Corner Patio

SPECIAL FEATURES

- 1,092 total square feet of living area
- Box window and inviting porch with dormers create a charming facade
- Eat-in kitchen offers a pass-through breakfast bar, corner window wall to patio, pantry and convenient laundry with half bath
- Master bedroom features double entry doors and walk-in closet
- 3 bedrooms, 1 1/2 baths, 1-car garage
- Basement foundation

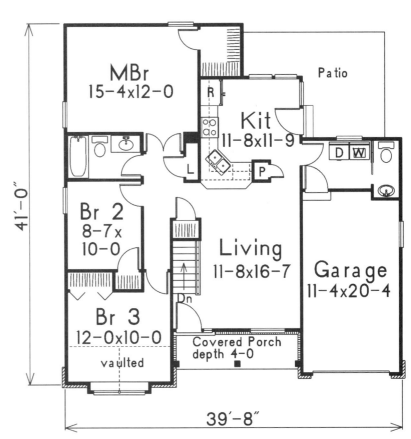

Floor-To-Ceiling *Window Expands* Compact Two-Story

SPECIAL FEATURES

- 1,246 total square feet of living area
- Corner living room window adds openness and light
- Out-of-the-way kitchen with dining area accesses the outdoors
- Private first floor master bedroom with corner window
- Large walk-in closet is located in bedroom #3
- Easily built perimeter allows economical construction
- 3 bedrooms, 2 baths, 2-car garage
- Basement foundation

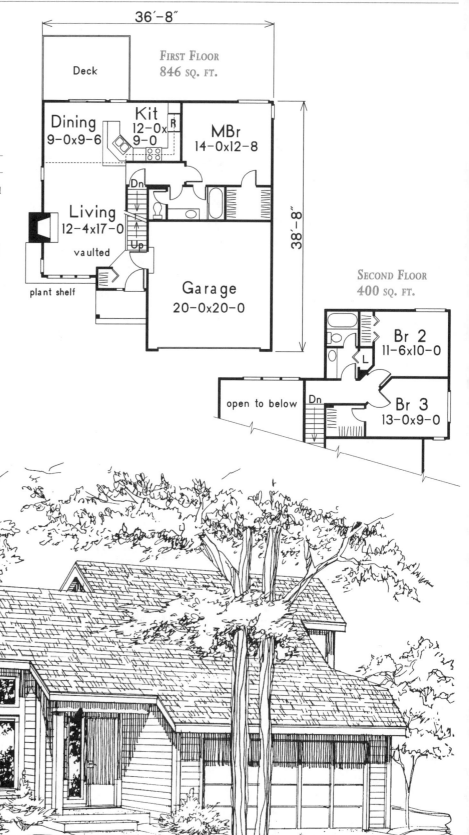

36'-8"

FIRST FLOOR
846 SQ. FT.

Deck

Dining
9-0x9-6

Kit
12-0x
9-0

MBr
14-0x12-8

Dn

Living
12-4x17-0

vaulted

Up

plant shelf

Garage
20-0x20-0

38'-8"

SECOND FLOOR
400 SQ. FT.

Br 2
11-6x10-0

L

open to below

Dn

Br 3
13-0x9-0

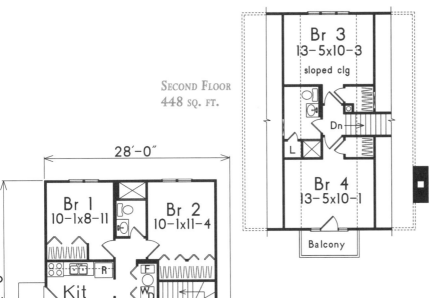

Second Floor
448 sq. ft.

Br 3
13-5x10-3
sloped clg

Dn

L

Br 4
13-5x10-1

Balcony

28'-0"

Br 1
10-1x8-11

Br 2
10-1x11-4

32'-0"

Kit
8-9x
10-1

F

W
D

Up

Dining
10-4x10-11

Living
14-11x13-4

First Floor
832 sq. ft.

Deck

A Chalet For Lakeside Living

SPECIAL FEATURES

- 1,280 total square feet of living area

- Attention to architectural detail has created the look of an authentic Swiss cottage

- Spacious living room including adjacent kitchenette and dining area, enjoy views to front deck

- Hall bath shared by two sizable bedrooms is included on first and second floors

- 4 bedrooms, 2 baths

- Crawl space foundation, drawings also include basement and slab foundations

Irresistible
Paradise Retreat

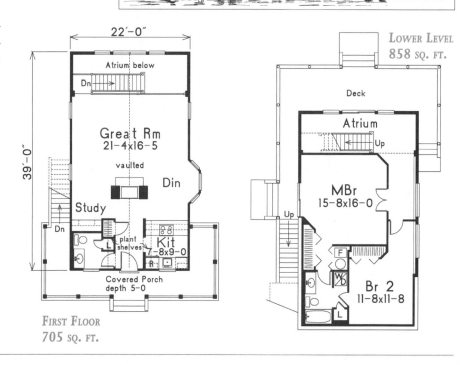

REAR VIEW

SPECIAL FEATURES

- 1,563 total square feet of living area

- Enjoyable wrap-around porch and lower sundeck

- Vaulted entry is adorned with palladian window, plant shelves, stone floor and fireplace

- Huge vaulted great room has magnificent views through a two-story atrium window wall

- 2 bedrooms, 1 1/2 baths

- Basement foundation

22'-0"

Atrium below

Dn

Great Rm
21-4x16-5

vaulted

Din

Study

39'-0"

Dn

plant shelves

Kit
7-8x9-0

Covered Porch
depth 5-0

FIRST FLOOR
705 SQ. FT.

LOWER LEVEL
858 SQ. FT.

Deck

Atrium

Up

MBr
15-8x16-0

Up

F

W D

Br 2
11-8x11-8

L

Plan #X22-0277

Price Code AA

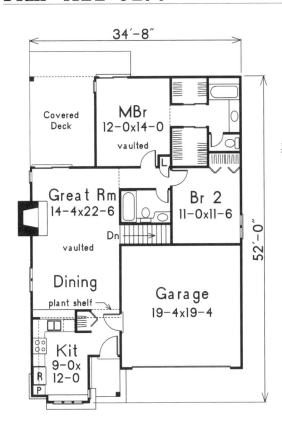

Charming Exterior And Cozy Interior

SPECIAL FEATURES

- 1,127 total square feet of living area
- Plant shelf joins kitchen and dining room
- Vaulted master suite has double walk-in closets, deck access and private bath
- Great room features vaulted ceiling, fireplace and sliding doors to covered deck
- Ideal home for a narrow lot
- 2 bedrooms, 2 baths, 2-car garage
- Basement foundation

Plan #X22-0462

Price Code AA

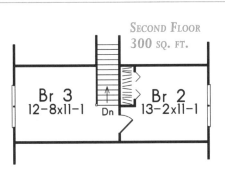

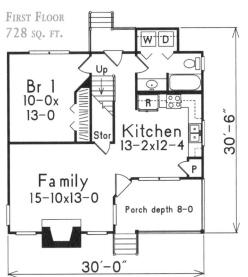

Quaint Country Home Is Ideal

SPECIAL FEATURES

- 1,028 total square feet of living area
- Master bedroom conveniently located on first floor
- Well-designed bath contains laundry facilities
- L-shaped kitchen has a handy pantry
- Tall windows flank family room fireplace
- Cozy covered porch provides unique angled entry into home
- 3 bedrooms, 1 bath
- Crawl space foundation

Three Bedroom Luxury In *A* Small Home

SPECIAL FEATURES

- 1,161 total square feet of living area
- Brickwork and feature window add elegance to home for a narrow lot
- Living room enjoys a vaulted ceiling, fireplace and opens to kitchen area
- U-shaped kitchen offers a breakfast area with bay window, snack bar and built-in pantry
- 3 bedrooms, 2 baths
- Basement foundation

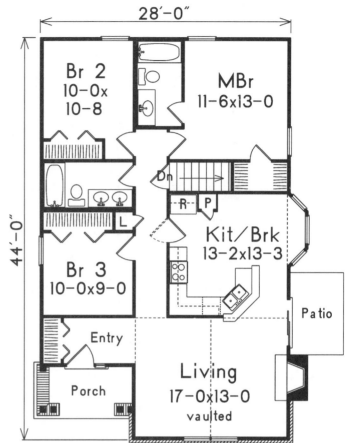

Unique A-Frame Detailing Has Appeal

SPECIAL FEATURES

- 1,272 total square feet of living area
- Stone fireplace accents living room
- Spacious kitchen includes snack bar overlooking living room
- First floor bedroom roomy and secluded
- Plenty of closet space for second floor bedrooms plus a generous balcony which wraps around second floor
- 3 bedrooms, 1 1/2 baths
- Crawl space foundation

Br 2
14-6x9-7

Br 3
14-6x11-5
sloped clg

Balcony

SECOND FLOOR
480 SQ. FT.

26'-4"

Deck

Br 1
15-0x10-1

Kit
8-9x 11-0

Living
20-4x11-6

48'-0"

Deck

FIRST FLOOR
792 SQ. FT.

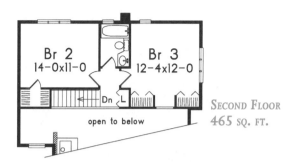

Br 2
14-0x11-0

Br 3
12-4x12-0

Dn L

open to below

SECOND FLOOR
465 SQ. FT.

Dramatic Sloping Ceiling In Living Room

SPECIAL FEATURES

- 1,432 total square feet of living area

- Enter into the two-story foyer from covered porch or garage

- Living room has square bay and window seat, glazed end wall with floor-to-ceiling windows and access to the deck

- Kitchen/dining room also opens to the deck for added convenience

- 3 bedrooms, 2 baths, 1-car garage

- Basement foundation, drawings also include slab foundation

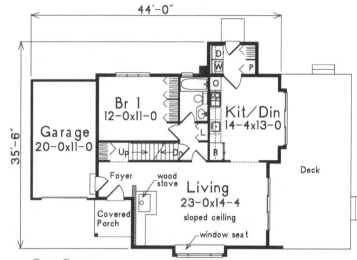

44'-0"

35'-6"

Garage
20-0x11-0

Br 1
12-0x11-0

Kit/Din
14-4x13-0

Up Dn

Foyer

wood stove

Living
23-0x14-4
sloped ceiling

Deck

Covered Porch

window seat

FIRST FLOOR
967 SQ. FT.

Cozy Ranch Home

SPECIAL FEATURES

- 950 total square feet of living area
- Deck adjacent to kitchen/breakfast area for outdoor dining
- Vaulted ceiling, open stairway and fireplace complement great room
- Secondary bedroom with sloped ceiling and box bay window can convert to den
- Master bedroom with walk-in closet, plant shelf, separate dressing area and private access to bath
- Kitchen has garage access and opens to great room
- 2 bedrooms, 1 bath, 1-car garage
- Basement foundation

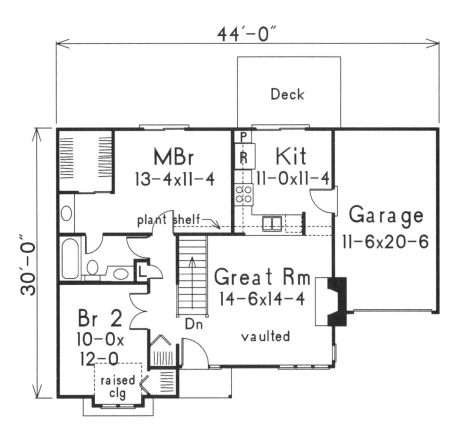

Double Dormers Accent This Cozy Vacation Retreat

SPECIAL FEATURES

- 581 total square feet of living area
- Living/dining room features a convenient kitchenette and spiral steps leading to the loft area
- Large loft space easily converted to a bedroom or work area
- Entry space has a unique built-in display niche
- 1 bedroom, 1 bath
- Slab foundation

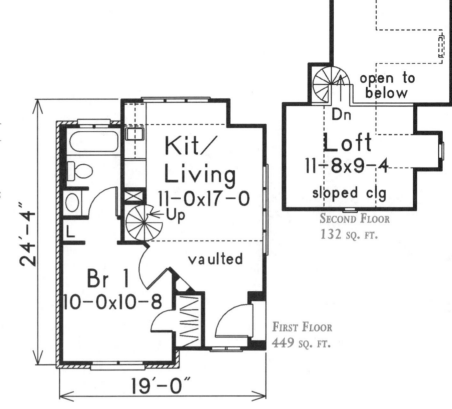

Kit/Living 11-0x17-0

Br 1 10-0x10-8

vaulted

24'-4"

19'-0"

Loft 11-8x9-4

sloped clg

open to below

Dn

Up

L

SECOND FLOOR 132 SQ. FT.

FIRST FLOOR 449 SQ. FT.

Deck

Kit
8-6x9-1

Dining
8-7x9-1

R

Dn | Up

plant shelf

37'-0"

Living
11-8x20-8
vaulted

Garage
11-5x23-5

Covered Porch
depth 6-4

24'-0"

FIRST FLOOR
545 SQ. FT.

Br 2
9-1x10-1

Dn

L

Br 1
11-5x11-2

SECOND FLOOR
432 SQ. FT.

Special Planning In This Compact Home

SPECIAL FEATURES

- 977 total square feet of living area

- Comfortable living room features a vaulted ceiling, fireplace, plant shelf and coat closet

- Both bedrooms are located on second floor and share a bath with double-bowl vanity and linen closet

- Sliding glass doors in dining room provide access to the deck

- 2 bedrooms, 1 1/2 baths, 1-car garage

- Basement foundation

Plan #X22-0651

Country Cottage Offers Vaulted Living

SPECIAL FEATURES

- 962 total square feet of living area
- Both the kitchen and family room share warmth from the fireplace
- Charming facade features covered porch on one side, screened porch on the other and attractive planter boxes
- L-shaped kitchen boasts convenient pantry
- 2 bedrooms, 1 bath
- Crawl space foundation

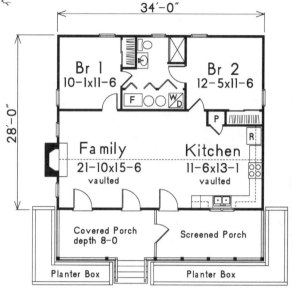

Plan #X22-0734

Three-Car Apartment Garage With Country Flair

SPECIAL FEATURES

- 929 total square feet of living area
- Spacious living room with dining area has access to 8' x 12' deck through glass sliding doors
- Splendid U-shaped kitchen features a breakfast bar, oval window above sink and impressive cabinet storage
- Master bedroom enjoys a walk-in closet and large elliptical feature window
- Laundry, storage closet and mechanical space are located off first floor garage
- 2 bedrooms, 1 bath, 3-car side entry garage
- Slab foundation

FIRST FLOOR 110 SQ. FT.

SECOND FLOOR 819 SQ. FT.

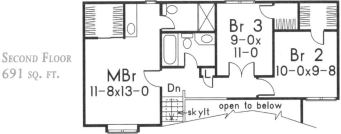

SECOND FLOOR
691 SQ. FT.

MBr
11-8x13-0

Br 3
9-0x
11-0

Br 2
10-0x9-8

Dn

skylt

open to below

Exterior Accents Add Charm To This Compact Cottage

SPECIAL FEATURES

- 1,359 total square feet of living area

- Lattice-trimmed porch, stone chimney and abundant windows lend outdoor appeal

- Spacious, bright breakfast area with pass-through to formal dining room

- Large walk-in closets in all bedrooms

- Extensive deck expands dining and entertaining areas

- 3 bedrooms, 2 1/2 baths, 2-car garage

- Basement foundation

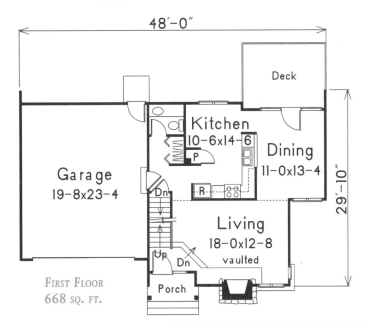

48'-0"

Deck

Kitchen
10-6x14-6

Dining
11-0x13-4

Garage
19-8x23-4

Dn

R

29'-10"

Living
18-0x12-8
vaulted

Up

Dn

Porch

FIRST FLOOR
668 SQ. FT.

Apartment Garage With Atrium

SPECIAL FEATURES

- 902 total square feet of living area

- Vaulted entry with laundry room leads to a spacious second floor apartment

- The large living room features an entry coat closet, L-shaped kitchen with pantry and dining area/balcony overlooking atrium window wall

- Roomy bedroom with walk-in closet is convenient to hall bath

- 1 bedroom, 1 bath, 2-car side entry garage

- Slab foundation

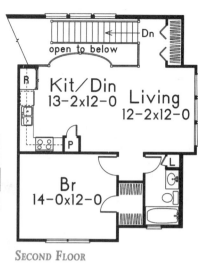

SECOND FLOOR
664 SQ. FT.

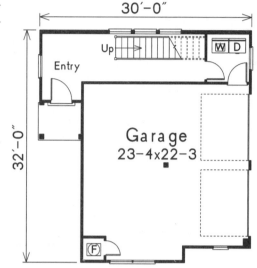

FIRST FLOOR
238 SQ. FT.

J.N. HANSEN S.D.G.

To order blueprints use the form on page 114 or call 1-800-DREAM HOME (373-2646)

Nestled Oasis Romances The Sun

SPECIAL FEATURES

- 1,584 total square feet of living area

- Vaulted living/dining room features stone fireplace, ascending spiral stair and separate vestibule with guest closet

- Space saving kitchen has an eat-in area and access to the deck

- Master bedroom adjoins a full bath

- 3 bedrooms, 2 baths

- Basement foundation, drawings also include crawl space and slab foundations

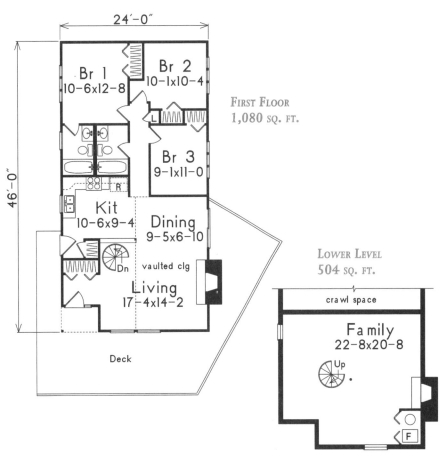

24'-0"

46'-0"

Br 1
10-6x12-8

Br 2
10-1x10-4

FIRST FLOOR
1,080 SQ. FT.

Br 3
9-1x11-0

Kit
10-6x9-4

Dining
9-5x6-10

vaulted clg

Dn

Living
17-4x14-2

Deck

LOWER LEVEL
504 SQ. FT.

crawl space

Family
22-8x20-8

Up

F

English Cottage With Modern Amenities

SPECIAL FEATURES

- 1,816 total square feet of living area

- Two-way living room fireplace with large nearby window seat

- Wrap-around dining room windows create sunroom appearance

- Master bedroom has abundant closet and storage space

- Rear dormers, closets and desk areas create interesting and functional second floor

- 3 bedrooms, 2 1/2 baths, 2-car detached garage

- Slab foundation, drawings also include crawl space foundation

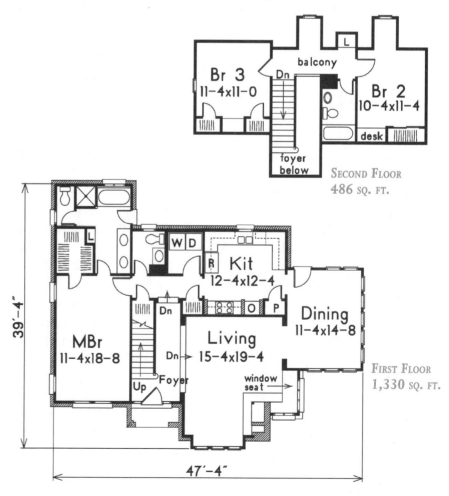

Br 3 11-4x11-0

balcony

Br 2 10-4x11-4

desk

foyer below

SECOND FLOOR 486 SQ. FT.

Kit 12-4x12-4

Dining 11-4x14-8

MBr 11-4x18-8

Living 15-4x19-4

window seat

Foyer

39'-4"

47'-4"

FIRST FLOOR 1,330 SQ. FT.

Plan #X22-N118

Price Code AAA

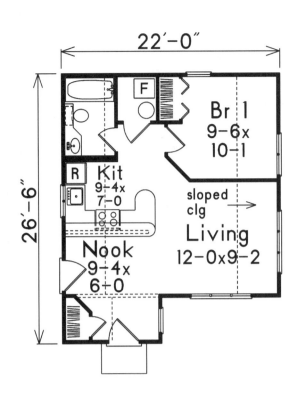

22'-0"

26'-6"

Br 1
9-6x
10-1

Kit
9-4x
7-0

Nook
9-4x
6-0

sloped clg

Living
12-0x9-2

F

R

Graciously Designed Refuge

SPECIAL FEATURES

- 527 total square feet of living area
- Cleverly arranged home has it all
- Foyer spills into the dining nook with access to side views
- An excellent kitchen offers a long breakfast bar and borders the living room with free-standing fireplace
- A cozy bedroom has a full bath just across the hall
- 1 bedroom, 1 bath
- Crawl space foundation

Plan #X22-N064

Price Code AA

Clerestory Windows Enhance Home's Facade

SPECIAL FEATURES

- 1,176 total square feet of living area
- Efficient kitchen offers plenty of storage, a dining area and a stylish eating bar
- A gathering space is created by the large central living room
- Closet and storage space throughout helps keep sporting equipment organized and easily accessible
- Each end of home is comprised of two bedrooms and full bath
- 4 bedrooms, 2 baths
- Crawl space foundation, drawings also include slab foundation

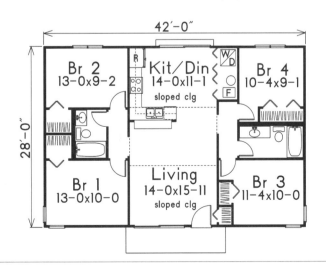

42'-0"

28'-0"

Br 2
13-0x9-2

Kit/Din
14-0x11-1
sloped clg

Br 4
10-4x9-1

W/D

R

F

Br 1
13-0x10-0

Living
14-0x15-11
sloped clg

Br 3
11-4x10-0

Plan #X22-0548

Price Code AA

Open Living Area

SPECIAL FEATURES

- 1,154 total square feet of living area

- U-shaped kitchen with large breakfast bar and handy laundry area

- Private second floor bedrooms share half bath

- Large living/dining area opens to deck

- 3 bedrooms, 1 1/2 baths

- Crawl space foundation, drawings also include slab foundation

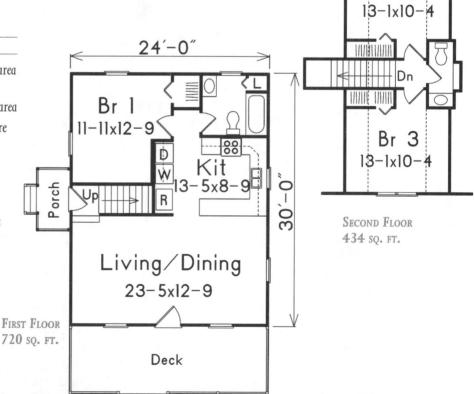

Br 2
13-1x10-4

Dn

Br 3
13-1x10-4

SECOND FLOOR
434 SQ. FT.

24'-0"

Br 1
11-11x12-9

30'-0"

Porch

Up

D
W
R

Kit
13-5x8-9

Living/Dining
23-5x12-9

FIRST FLOOR
720 SQ. FT.

Deck

To order blueprints use the form on page 114 or call 1-800-DREAM HOME (373-2646)

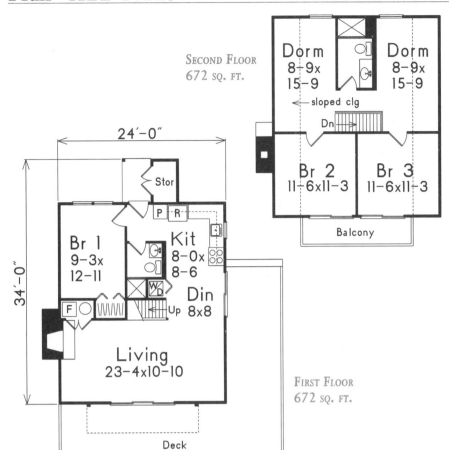

SECOND FLOOR
672 SQ. FT.

Dorm
8-9x
15-9

Dorm
8-9x
15-9

← sloped clg

Dn

Br 2
11-6x11-3

Br 3
11-6x11-3

Balcony

24'-0"

Stor

P R

Br 1
9-3x
12-11

Kit
8-0x
8-6

34'-0"

W D

Din
8x8

Up

F

Living
23-4x10-10

FIRST FLOOR
672 SQ. FT.

Deck

Irresistible Cottage Adorns Any Setting

SPECIAL FEATURES

- 1,344 total square feet of living area

- Beautiful stone fireplace, bracketed balcony and surrounding deck create appealing atmosphere

- Enormous living room, open to dining area, enjoys views to deck through two large sliding doors

- Second floor delivers lots of sleeping area and views from exterior balcony

- 5 bedrooms, 2 baths

- Crawl space foundation, drawings also include slab foundation

Plan #X22-0699

Comfortable Vacation Retreat

SPECIAL FEATURES

- 1,073 total square feet of living area
- Home includes lovely covered front porch and a screened porch off dining area
- Attractive box window brightens kitchen
- Space for efficiency washer and dryer located conveniently between bedrooms
- Family room spotlighted by fireplace with flanking bookshelves and spacious vaulted ceiling
- 2 bedrooms, 1 bath
- Crawl space foundation

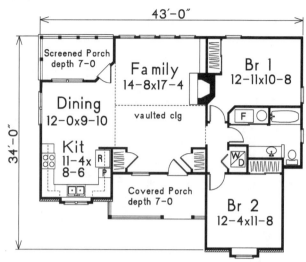

Plan #X22-0757

Compact Home For Sloping Lot

SPECIAL FEATURES

- 1,332 total square feet of living area
- Home offers both basement and first floor entry locations
- A dramatic living room features a vaulted ceiling, fireplace, exterior balcony and dining area
- An L-shaped kitchen offers spacious cabinetry, breakfast area with bay window and access to rear patio
- 3 bedrooms, 2 baths, 4-car tandem basement garage
- Walk-out basement foundation

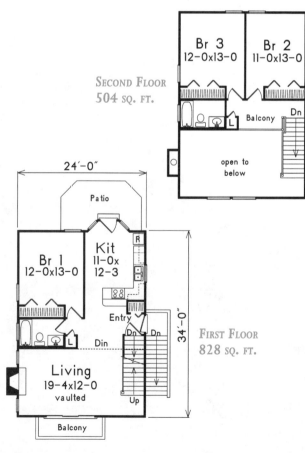

Compact Home, Perfect Fit For Narrow Lot

SPECIAL FEATURES

- 1,085 total square feet of living area
- Rear porch is a handy access through the kitchen
- Convenient hall linen closet located on the second floor
- Breakfast bar in kitchen offers additional counterspace
- Living and dining rooms combine for an open living atmosphere
- 3 bedrooms, 2 baths
- Basement foundation

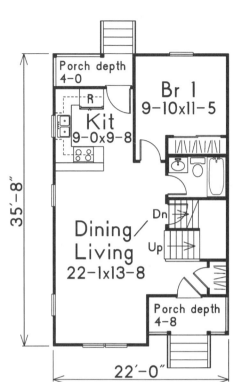

Porch depth 4-0

R

Kit
9-0x9-8

Br 1
9-10x11-5

Dining/
Living
22-1x13-8

Dn

Up

35'-8"

Porch depth 4-8

22'-0"

FIRST FLOOR
685 SQ. FT.

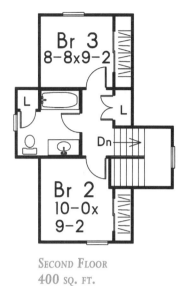

Br 3
8-8x9-2

L

L

Dn

Br 2
10-0x
9-2

SECOND FLOOR
400 SQ. FT.

Roomy
Vacation Retreat

SPECIAL FEATURES

- 2,652 total square feet of living area

- Multiple levels provide many areas for entertaining

- Oversized living room features enormous fireplace

- Large balcony ideal for admiring views

- Compact, yet efficient kitchen includes breakfast bar

- Plenty of closet space for sports equipment and patio furniture storage

- 3 bedrooms, 2 1/2 baths and 2-car garage

- Basement foundation

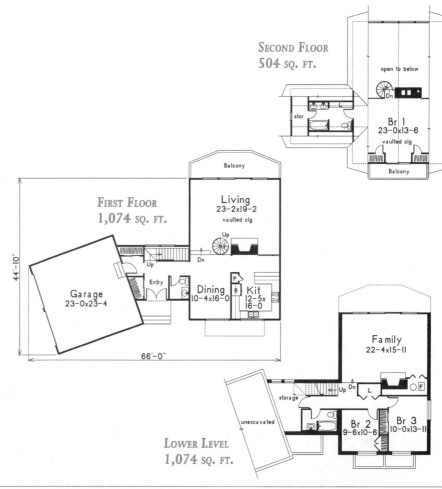

SECOND FLOOR
504 SQ. FT.

open to below

stor

Br 1
23-0x13-6
vaulted clg

Balcony

FIRST FLOOR
1,074 SQ. FT.

Balcony

Living
23-2x19-2
vaulted clg

Up

Dn

44'-10"

Garage
23-0x23-4

Entry

Dining
10-4x16-0

Kit
12-5x
16-0

66'-0"

Family
22-4x15-11

storage

Up Dn

unexcavated

Br 2
9-6x10-6

Br 3
10-0x13-11

LOWER LEVEL
1,074 SQ. FT.

Plan #X22-0695

Price Code AAA

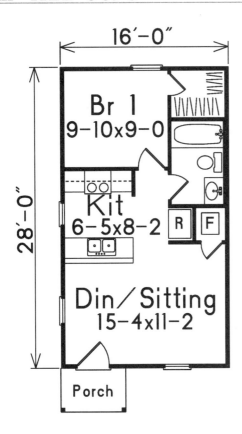

Irresistible Retreat

SPECIAL FEATURES

- 448 total square feet of living area
- Bedroom features large walk-in closet ideal for storage
- Combined dining/living area ideal for relaxing
- Galley-style kitchen is compact and efficient
- Covered porch adds to front facade
- 1 bedroom, 1 bath
- Slab foundation

Plan #X22-N010

Price Code AAA

Designed For Seclusion

SPECIAL FEATURES

- 624 total square feet of living area
- Combine stone, vertical siding, and lots of glass; add low roof line and you have a cozy retreat
- Vaulted living area features free-standing fireplace that heats adjacent stone wall for warmth
- Efficient kitchen includes dining area and view to angular deck
- Two bedrooms share a hall bath with shower
- 2 bedrooms, 1 bath
- Pier foundation

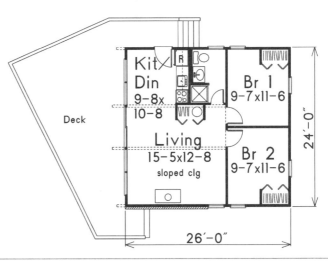

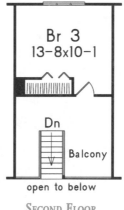

Br 3
13-8x10-1

Dn

Balcony

open to below

SECOND FLOOR
328 SQ. FT.

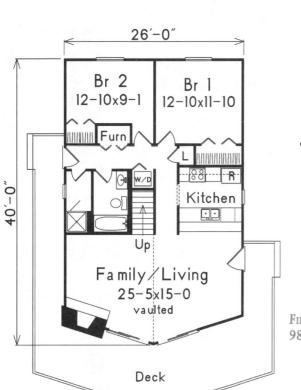

26'-0"

Br 2
12-10x9-1

Br 1
12-10x11-10

Furn

W/D

L

R

Kitchen

Up

Family/Living
25-5x15-0
vaulted

40'-0"

Deck

FIRST FLOOR
988 SQ. FT.

Unique Yet Functional Design

SPECIAL FEATURES

- 1,316 total square feet of living area

- Massive vaulted family/living room is accented with fireplace and views to outdoors through sliding glass doors

- Galley-style kitchen is centrally located

- Unique separate shower room near bath doubles as a convenient mud room

- 3 bedrooms, 1 bath

- Crawl space foundation

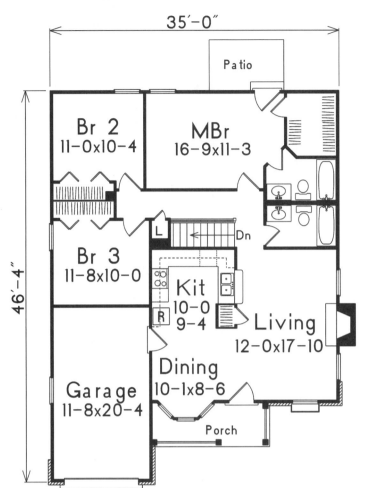

35'-0"

Patio

Br 2
11-0x10-4

MBr
16-9x11-3

46'-4"

Br 3
11-8x10-0

L   Dn

Kit
10-0
9-4

Living
12-0x17-10

Dining
10-1x8-6

Garage
11-8x20-4

Porch

Country Charm
For A Small Lot

SPECIAL FEATURES

- 1,169 total square feet of living area
- Front facade features a distinctive country appeal
- Living room enjoys a wood-burning fireplace and pass-through to kitchen
- A stylish U-shaped kitchen offers an abundance of cabinet and counterspace with view to living room
- A large walk-in closet, access to rear patio and private bath are many features of the master bedroom
- 3 bedrooms, 2 baths, 1-car garage
- Basement foundation

A Vacation Oasis

SPECIAL FEATURES

- 1,026 total square feet of living area
- Delightful A-frame provides exciting vacation all year long
- Sundeck accesses large living room with open soaring ceiling
- Enormous sleeping area is provided on second floor with balcony overlook of living room below
- 2 bedrooms, 1 bath
- Pier foundation

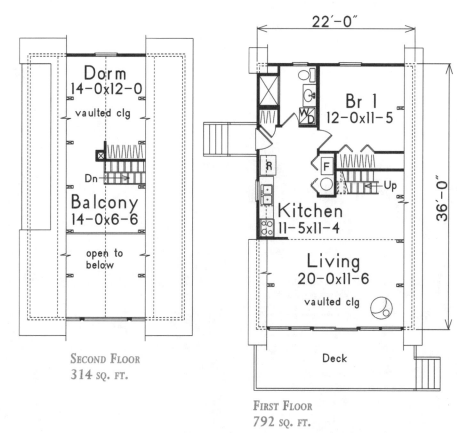

Dorm
14-0x12-0
vaulted clg

Dn

Balcony
14-0x6-6

open to below

SECOND FLOOR
314 SQ. FT.

22'-0"

Br 1
12-0x11-5

36'-0"

R

F

Up

W
D

Kitchen
11-5x11-4

Living
20-0x11-6
vaulted clg

Deck

FIRST FLOOR
792 SQ. FT.

Compact, Convenient And Charming

SPECIAL FEATURES

- 1,266 total square feet of living area

- Narrow frontage is perfect for small lots

- Energy efficient home with 2" x 6" exterior walls

- Prominent central hall provides a convenient connection for all main rooms

- Design incorporates full-size master bedroom complete with dressing room, bath and walk-in closet

- Angled kitchen includes handy laundry facilities and is adjacent to an oversized storage area

- 3 bedrooms, 2 baths, 2-car rear entry garage

- Crawl space foundation, drawings also include slab foundation

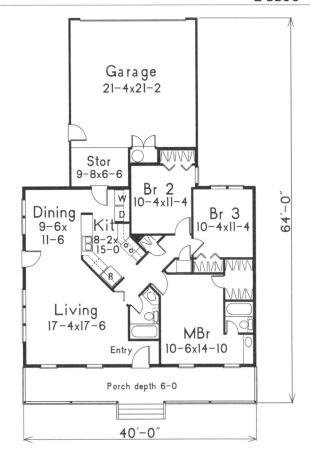

Plan #X22-N087

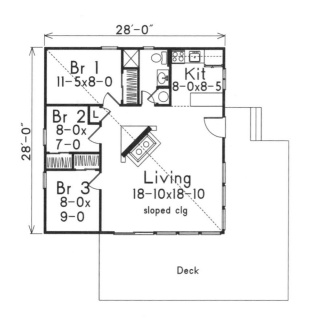

Corner Window Wall Dominates Design

SPECIAL FEATURES

- 784 total square feet of living area
- Outdoor relaxation will be enjoyed with this home's huge wrap-around wood deck
- Upon entering the spacious living area, a cozy free-standing fireplace, sloped ceiling and corner window wall catch the eye
- Charming pullman-style kitchen features pass-through peninsula to dining area
- 3 bedrooms, 1 bath
- Pier foundation

Plan #X22-0698

Price Code AA

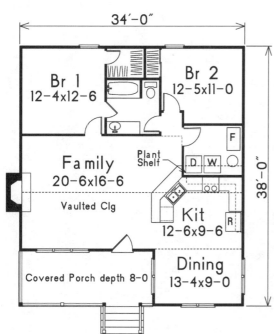

Flexible Layout For Various Uses

SPECIAL FEATURES

- 1,143 total square feet of living area
- Enormous stone fireplace in family room adds warmth and character
- Spacious kitchen with breakfast bar overlooks family room
- Separate dining area great for entertaining
- Vaulted family room and kitchen create an open atmosphere
- 2 bedrooms, 1 bath
- Crawl space foundation

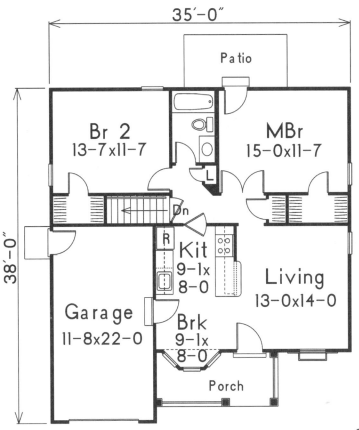

35'-0"

Patio

Br 2
13-7x11-7

MBr
15-0x11-7

38'-0"

Dn

Kit
9-1x
8-0

Living
13-0x14-0

R

Garage
11-8x22-0

Brk
9-1x
8-0

Porch

Elegance In A Starter Or Retirement Home

SPECIAL FEATURES

- 888 total square feet of living area
- Home features an eye-catching exterior and includes a spacious porch
- The breakfast room with bay window is open to living room and adjoins kitchen with pass-through snack bar
- The bedrooms are quite roomy and feature walk-in closets and the master bedroom has double entry doors and access to rear patio
- The master bedroom has double entry doors and access to rear patio
- 2 bedrooms, 1 bath, 1-car garage
- Basement foundation

Great Room Window Adds Character Inside And Out

SPECIAL FEATURES

- 1,368 total square feet of living area
- Entry foyer steps down to open living area which combines great room and formal dining area
- Vaulted master suite includes box bay window, large vanity, separate tub and shower
- Cozy breakfast area features direct access to the patio and pass-through kitchen
- Handy linen closet located in hall
- 3 bedrooms, 2 baths, 2-car garage
- Basement foundation

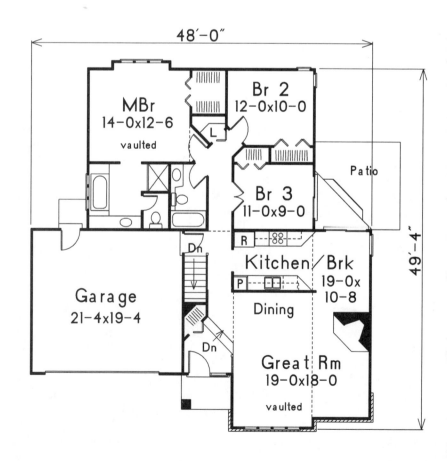

Cozy Vacation Retreat

SPECIAL FEATURES

- 1,391 total square feet of living area
- Large living room with masonry fireplace features soaring vaulted ceiling
- A spiral staircase in hall leads to huge loft area overlooking living room below
- Two first floor bedrooms share a full bath
- 2 bedrooms, 1 bath
- Pier foundation, drawings also include crawl space foundation

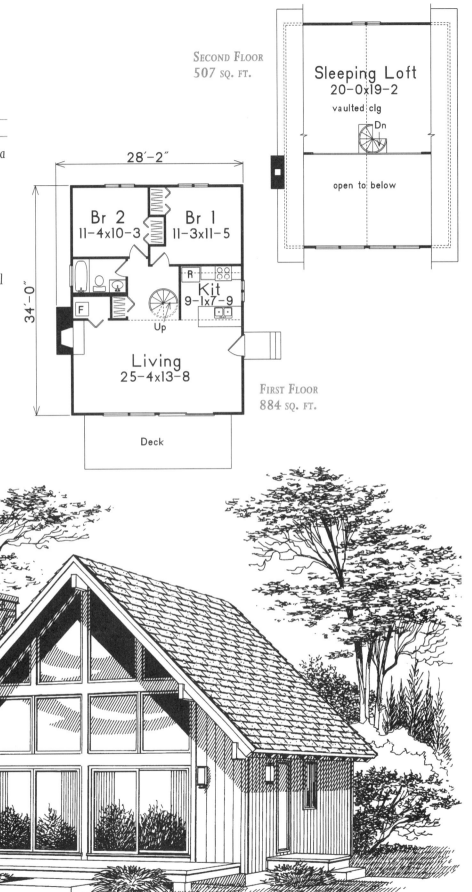

SECOND FLOOR
507 SQ. FT.

Sleeping Loft
20-0x19-2
vaulted clg

Dn

open to below

28′-2″

Br 2
11-4x10-3

Br 1
11-3x11-5

R

Kit
9-1x7-9

Up

34′-0″

F

Living
25-4x13-8

FIRST FLOOR
884 SQ. FT.

Deck

Large Corner Deck Lends Way To Outdoor Living Area

SPECIAL FEATURES

- 1,283 total square feet of living area
- Vaulted breakfast room with sliding doors that open onto deck
- Kitchen features convenient corner sink and pass-through to dining room
- Open living atmosphere in dining area and great room
- Vaulted great room features a fireplace
- 3 bedrooms, 2 baths, 2-car garage
- Basement foundation

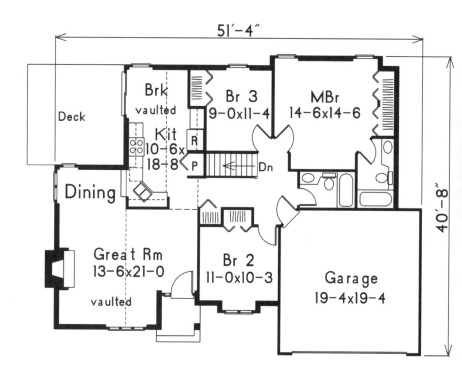

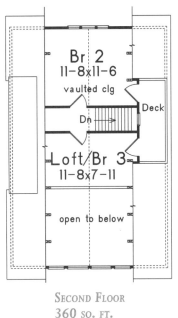

Br 2
11-8x11-6
vaulted clg

Deck

Dn

Loft/Br 3
11-8x7-11

open to below

SECOND FLOOR
360 SQ. FT.

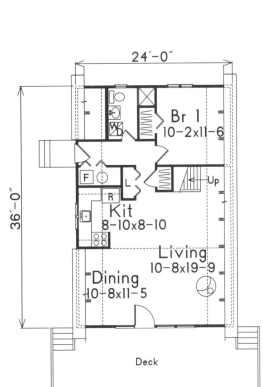

24'-0"

Br 1
10-2x11-6

36'-0"

Up

F

L

R

Kit
8-10x8-10

Living
10-8x19-9

Dining
10-8x11-5

Deck

FIRST FLOOR
864 SQ. FT.

Fantastic A-Frame Get-Away

SPECIAL FEATURES

- 1,224 total square feet of living area

- *Get away to this cozy A-frame featuring three bedrooms*

- *Living/dining room with free-standing fireplace walks out onto a large deck*

- *U-shaped kitchen has a unique built-in table at end of counter for intimate gatherings*

- *Both second floor bedrooms enjoy their own private balcony*

- *3 bedrooms, 1 bath*

- *Crawl space foundation*

Vacation Retreat With Attractive A-Frame Styling

SPECIAL FEATURES

- 1,312 total square feet of living area
- Expansive deck extends directly off living area
- L-shaped kitchen is organized and efficient
- Bedroom to the left of the kitchen makes a great quiet retreat or office
- Living area flanked with windows for light
- 3 bedrooms, 1 1/2 baths
- Pier foundation

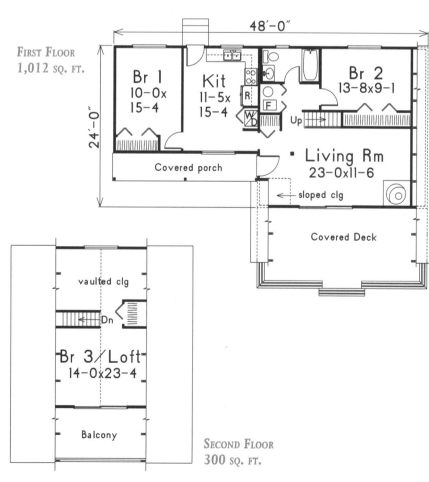

FIRST FLOOR
1,012 SQ. FT.

48'-0"

24'-0"

Br 1
10-0x
15-4

Kit
11-5x
15-4

Br 2
13-8x9-1

R

F

W
D

Up

Covered porch

Living Rm
23-0x11-6

sloped clg

Covered Deck

vaulted clg

Dn

Br 3/Loft
14-0x23-4

Balcony

SECOND FLOOR
300 SQ. FT.

Distinctive Ranch Has A Larger Look

SPECIAL FEATURES

- 1,360 total square feet of living area
- Double-gabled front facade frames large windows
- Entry area is open to vaulted great room, fireplace and rear deck creating an open feel
- Vaulted ceiling and large windows add openness to kitchen/breakfast room
- Bedroom #3 easily converts to a den
- Plan easily adapts to crawl space or slab construction, with the utilities replacing the stairs
- 3 bedrooms, 2 baths, 2-car garage
- Basement foundation

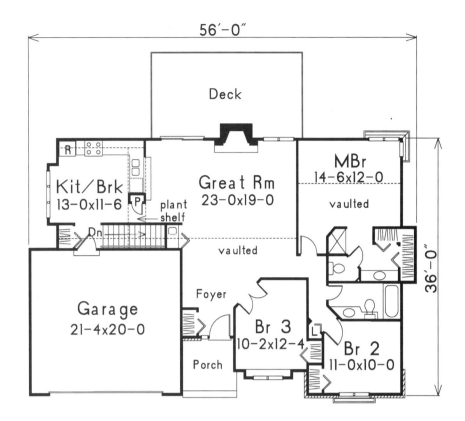

Country Kitchen Center Of Living Activities

SPECIAL FEATURES

- 1,556 total square feet of living area
- A compact home with all the amenities
- Country kitchen combines practicality with access to other areas for eating and entertaining
- Two-way fireplace joins the dining and living areas
- Plant shelf and vaulted ceiling highlight the master bedroom
- 3 bedrooms, 2 1/2 baths, 2-car garage
- Basement foundation

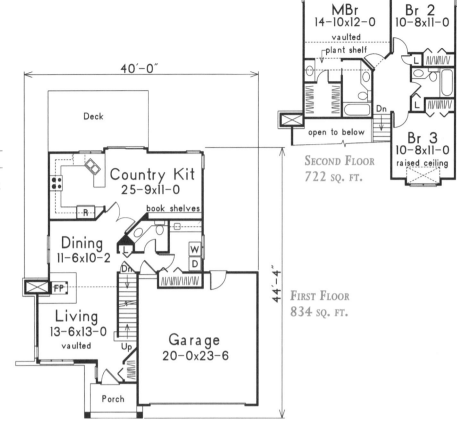

SECOND FLOOR 722 SQ. FT.

FIRST FLOOR 834 SQ. FT.

Plan #X22-0582

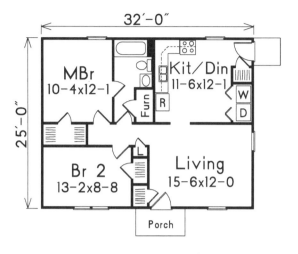

Ideal Starter Home

SPECIAL FEATURES

- 800 total square feet of living area
- Master bedroom has walk-in closet and private access to bath
- Large living room features handy coat closet
- Kitchen includes side entrance, closet and convenient laundry area
- 2 bedrooms, 1 bath
- Crawl space foundation, drawings also include basement and slab foundations

Plan #X22-0241

Price Code AAA

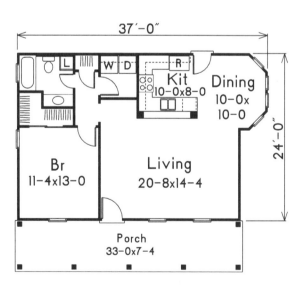

Large Front Porch Adds Welcoming Appeal

SPECIAL FEATURES

- 829 total square feet of living area
- U-shaped kitchen opens into living area by a 42" high counter
- Oversized bay window and French door accent dining room
- Gathering space is created by the large living room
- Convenient utility room and linen closet
- 1 bedroom, 1 bath
- Slab foundation

Perfect Fit
For A Narrow Site

SPECIAL FEATURES

- 1,270 total square feet of living area

- Spacious living area features angled stairs, vaulted ceiling, exciting fireplace and deck access

- Master bedroom includes a walk-in closet and private bath

- Dining and living rooms join to create an open atmosphere

- Eat-in kitchen with convenient pass-through to dining room

- 3 bedrooms, 2 baths, 2-car garage

- Basement foundation

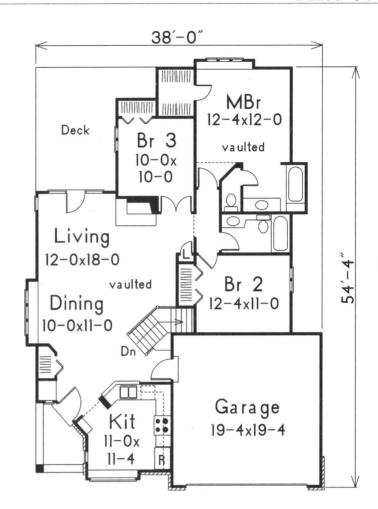

Second Floor
420 SQ. FT.

Br 2
13-1x10-1

Dn

Br 3
13-1x13-6
← sloped clg

Balcony

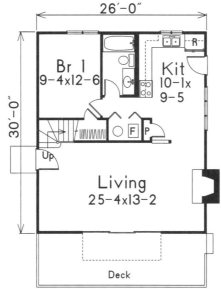

First Floor
780 SQ. FT.

26'-0"

Br 1
9-4x12-6

Kit
10-1x
9-5

30'-0"

Up

Living
25-4x13-2

Deck

Roughing
It In Luxury

SPECIAL FEATURES

- 1,200 total square feet of living area

- Ornate ranch-style railing enhances exterior while the stone fireplace provides a visual anchor

- Spectacular living room features inviting fireplace and adjoins a charming kitchen with dining area

- First floor bedroom, hall bath and two second floor bedrooms with half bath and exterior balcony complete the home

- 3 bedrooms, 1 1/2 baths

- Crawl space foundation, drawings also include slab foundation

Plan #X22-0476

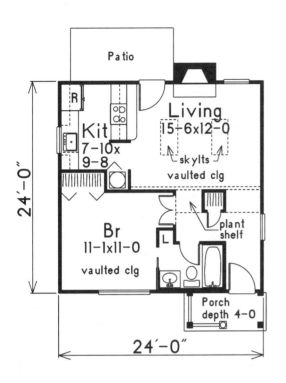

A Cottage With Class

SPECIAL FEATURES

- 576 total square feet of living area
- Perfect country retreat features vaulted living room and entry with skylights and plant shelf above
- Double-doors enter a vaulted bedroom with bath access
- Kitchen offers generous storage and pass-through breakfast bar
- 1 bedroom, 1 bath
- Crawl space foundation

Plan #X22-0697

Price Code AA

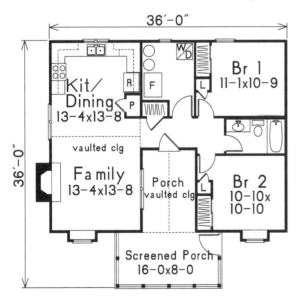

Excellent For Weekend Entertaining

SPECIAL FEATURES

- 924 total square feet of living area
- Box bay window seats brighten interior while enhancing front facade
- Spacious kitchen with lots of cabinet space and large pantry
- T-shaped covered porch is screened in for added enjoyment
- Plenty of closet space throughout with linen closets in both bedrooms
- 2 bedrooms, 1 bath
- Slab foundation

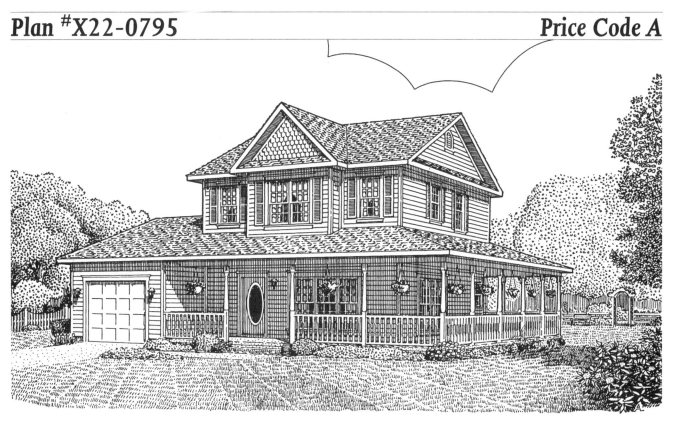

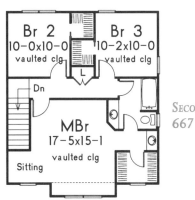

Br 2
10-0x10-0
vaulted clg

Br 3
10-2x10-0
vaulted clg

Dn

MBr
17-5x15-1
vaulted clg

Sitting

SECOND FLOOR
667 SQ. FT.

Covered Porch Surrounds Home

SPECIAL FEATURES

- 1,399 total square feet of living area

- Living room overlooks dining area through arched columns

- Laundry room contains handy half bath

- Spacious master bedroom includes sitting area, walk-in closet and plenty of sunlight

- 3 bedrooms, 1 1/2 baths, 1-car garage

- Basement foundation, drawings also include crawl space and slab foundations

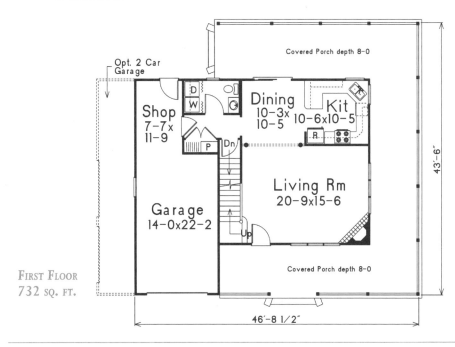

Opt. 2 Car Garage

Covered Porch depth 8-0

Shop
7-7x
11-9

Dining
10-3x
10-5

Kit
10-6x10-5

Dn

Living Rm
20-9x15-6

Garage
14-0x22-2

43'-6"

Covered Porch depth 8-0

46'-8 1/2"

FIRST FLOOR
732 SQ. FT.

Master Suite
Spacious And Private

SPECIAL FEATURES

- 1,160 total square feet of living area
- Kitchen/dining area combines with laundry area creating a functional organized area
- Spacious vaulted living area has large fireplace and is brightened by glass doors accessing large deck
- Ascend to second floor loft by spiral stairs and find a cozy hideaway
- Master suite brightened by many windows and includes private bath and double closets
- 1 bedroom, 1 bath
- Crawl space foundation

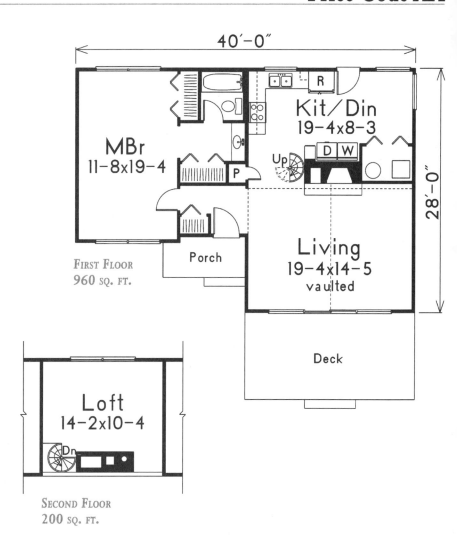

FIRST FLOOR
960 SQ. FT.

SECOND FLOOR
200 SQ. FT.

Br 3
9-2x13-9

Br 2
10-3x13-9

L

Dn

L

open to below

SECOND FLOOR
429 SQ. FT.

Mountain Retreat

SPECIAL FEATURES

- 1,209 total square feet of living area
- Bracketed shed roof and ski storage add charm to vacation home
- Living and dining rooms enjoy sloped ceilings, second floor balcony overlook and view to large deck
- Kitchen features snack bar and access to second floor via circular stair
- Second floor includes two bedrooms with sizable closets, center hall bath and balcony overlooking rooms below
- 3 bedrooms, 2 baths
- Crawl space foundation

29'-0"

stor

Ski Hall
9-2x8-9

W D

L

Br 1
10-3x12-11

R

Kit
7-0x7-4

Up

F

30'-0"

Living
15-4x12-11
sloped clg

FIRST FLOOR
780 SQ. FT.

Deck

Compact Home Maximizes Space

SPECIAL FEATURES

- 987 total square feet of living area
- Galley kitchen opens into cozy breakfast room
- Convenient coat closets located by both entrances
- Dining/living room combined for expansive open area
- Breakfast room has access to the outdoors
- Front porch great for enjoying outdoor living
- 3 bedrooms, 1 bath
- Basement foundation

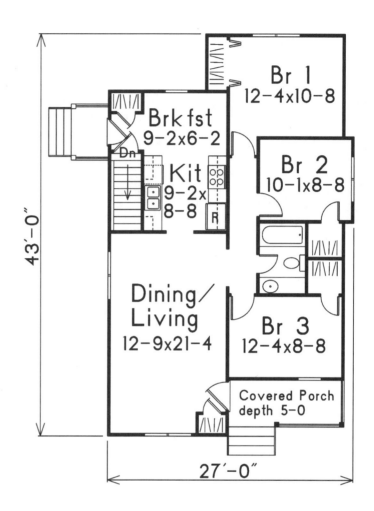

To order blueprints use the form on page 114 or call 1-800-DREAM HOME (373-2646)

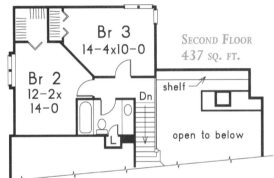

Br 3
14-4x10-0

SECOND FLOOR
437 SQ. FT.

Br 2
12-2x
14-0

Dn

shelf

open to below

L

Gabled Front Porch Adds Charm And Value

SPECIAL FEATURES

- 1,443 total square feet of living area
- Raised foyer and cathedral ceiling in living room
- Impressive tall-wall fireplace between living and dining rooms
- Open U-shaped kitchen with breakfast bay
- Angular side deck accentuates patio and garden
- First floor master bedroom suite has a walk-in closet and a corner window
- 3 bedrooms, 2 baths, 2-car garage
- Basement foundation

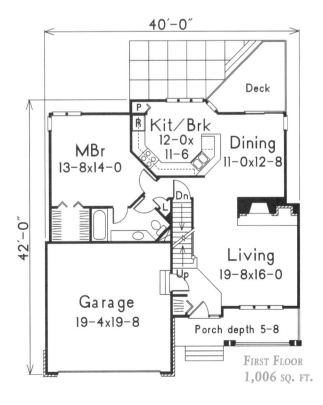

40'-0"

42'-0"

Deck

P
R

Kit/Brk
12-0x
11-6

Dining
11-0x12-8

MBr
13-8x14-0

Dn
L

Up

Living
19-8x16-0

Garage
19-4x19-8

Porch depth 5-8

FIRST FLOOR
1,006 SQ. FT.

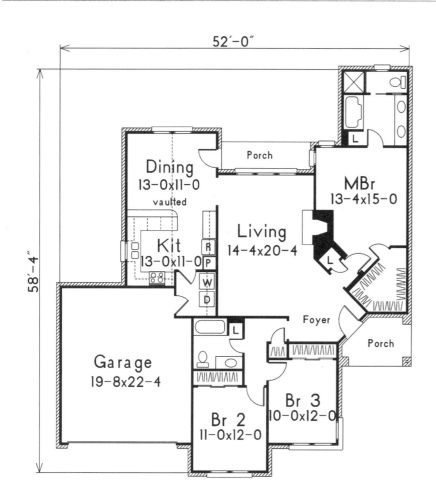

Dining
13-0x11-0
vaulted

Porch

MBr
13-4x15-0

Kit
13-0x11-0

R
P

Living
14-4x20-4

W
D

L

Foyer

Garage
19-8x22-4

L

Porch

Br 3
10-0x12-0

Br 2
11-0x12-0

52'-0"

58'-4"

Sheltered Entrance Opens To Stylish Features

SPECIAL FEATURES

- 1,661 total square feet of living area
- Large open foyer with angled wall arrangement and high ceiling adds to spacious living room
- Dining/kitchen area has impressive cathedral ceiling and French door allowing access to the patio
- Utility room conveniently located near kitchen
- Secluded master bedroom has large walk-in closets, unique brick wall arrangement and 10' ceiling
- 3 bedrooms, 2 baths, 2-car garage
- Slab foundation

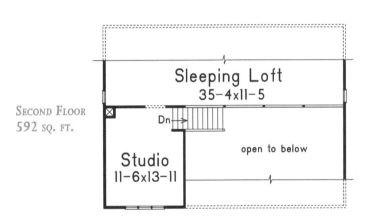

SECOND FLOOR
592 SQ. FT.

Sleeping Loft
35-4x11-5

Dn

open to below

Studio
11-6x13-11

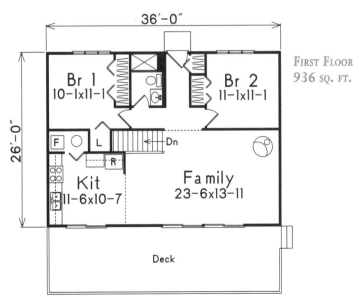

36'-0"

26'-0"

Br 1
10-1x11-1

Br 2
11-1x11-1

F
L
R
Dn

Kit
11-6x10-7

Family
23-6x13-11

FIRST FLOOR
936 SQ. FT.

Deck

Trendsetting Contemporary Retreat

SPECIAL FEATURES

- 1,528 total square feet of living area

- Large deck complements handsome exterior

- Family room provides a welcome space for family get-togethers and includes a sloped ceiling and access to studio/loft

- Kitchen features dining space and view to deck

- A hall bath is shared by two bedrooms on first floor which have ample closet space

- 2 bedrooms, 1 bath

- Crawl space foundation

Plan #X22-0693

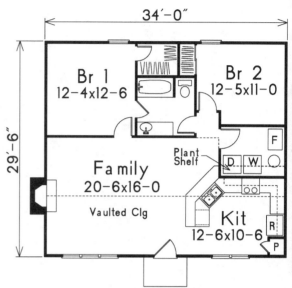

Ideal Home Or Retirement Retreat

SPECIAL FEATURES

- 1,013 total square feet of living area
- Vaulted ceiling in both family room and kitchen with dining area just beyond breakfast bar
- Plant shelf above kitchen is a special feature
- Oversized utility room has space for full-size washer and dryer
- Hall bath is centrally located with easy access from both bedrooms
- 2 bedrooms, 1 bath
- Slab foundation

Plan #X22-0764

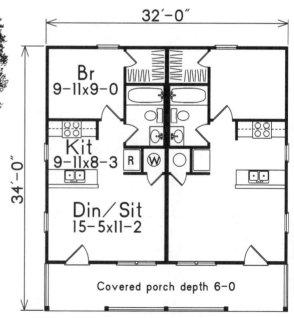

Efficient And Open Duplex Design

SPECIAL FEATURES

- 896 total square feet of living area
- Small cabin duplex well-suited for rental property or permanent residence
- Compact, yet convenient floor plan
- Well-organized for economical construction
- Each unit has 1 bedroom, 1 bath
- Slab foundation
- Duplex has 448 square feet of living space per unit

Contemporary Design For Open Family Living

SPECIAL FEATURES

- 1,516 total square feet of living area

- All living and dining areas are interconnected for a spacious look and easy movement

- Covered entrance leads into sunken great room with a rugged corner fireplace

- Family kitchen combines practicality with access to other areas

- Second floor loft, opens to rooms below, converts to third bedroom

- Dormer in bedroom 2 adds interest

- 3 bedrooms, 2 1/2 baths, 2-car garage

- Basement foundation

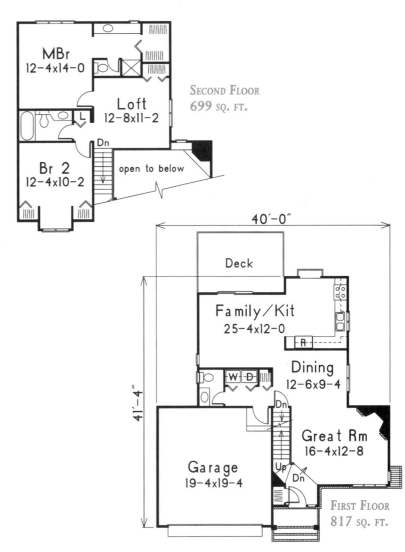

MBr
12-4x14-0

Loft
12-8x11-2

SECOND FLOOR
699 SQ. FT.

Br 2
12-4x10-2

Dn

open to below

40'-0"

Deck

Family/Kit
25-4x12-0

R

Dining
12-6x9-4

41'-4"

W D

Dn

Great Rm
16-4x12-8

Garage
19-4x19-4

Up

Dn

FIRST FLOOR
817 SQ. FT.

Plan #X22-N109

Price Code C

A Home Designed For Hillside Views

SPECIAL FEATURES

- 1,806 total square feet of living area
- Wrap-around deck, great for entertaining, enhances appearance
- Side entry foyer accesses two rear bedrooms, hall bath and living and dining area
- L-shaped kitchen is open to dining area
- Lots of living area is provided on the lower level, including a spacious family room with fireplace and sliding doors to patio under deck
- 3 bedrooms, 2 baths
- Basement foundation

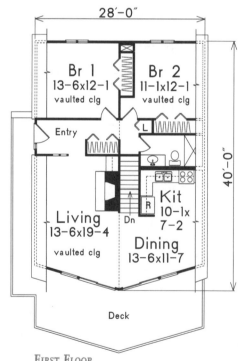

28'-0"

40'-0"

Br 1
13-6x12-1
vaulted clg

Br 2
11-1x12-1
vaulted clg

Entry

Living
13-6x19-4
vaulted clg

Dn

Kit
10-1x
7-2

Dining
13-6x11-7

Deck

FIRST FLOOR
1,064 SQ. FT.

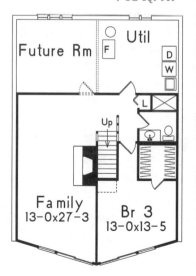

LOWER LEVEL
742 SQ. FT.

Future Rm

Util

Family
13-0x27-3

Br 3
13-0x13-5

Up

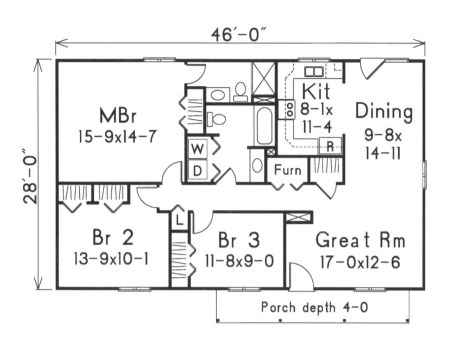

46'-0"

MBr
15-9x14-7

28'-0"

Kit
8-1x
11-4

Dining
9-8x
14-11

W
D

Furn

Br 2
13-9x10-1

L

Br 3
11-8x9-0

Great Rm
17-0x12-6

Porch depth 4-0

Peaceful Shaded Front Porch

SPECIAL FEATURES

- 1,288 total square feet of living area
- Kitchen, dining area and great room join to create an open living space
- Master bedroom includes private bath
- Secondary bedrooms include ample closet space
- Hall bath features convenient laundry closet
- Dining room accesses the outdoors
- 3 bedrooms, 2 baths
- Crawl space foundation, drawings also include basement and slab foundations

Plan #X22-N005

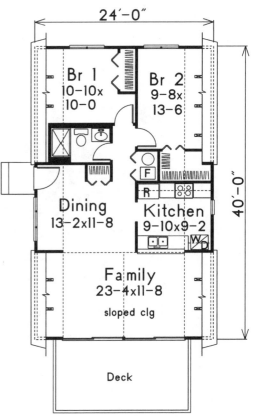

Vacation Paradise

SPECIAL FEATURES

- 960 total square feet of living area
- Interesting roof and wood beams overhang a generous-sized deck
- Family/living area is vaulted and opens to dining and kitchen
- Pullman-style kitchen has been skillfully designed
- Two bedrooms and hall bath are located at the rear of home
- 2 bedrooms, 1 bath
- Crawl space foundation

Plan #X22-0461

Price Code AAA

Cottage-Style, Appealing And Cozy

SPECIAL FEATURES

- 828 total square feet of living area
- Vaulted ceiling in living area enhances space
- Covered entry porch provides cozy sitting area and plenty of shade
- Sloped ceiling creates unique style in bedroom #2
- Efficient storage space under the stairs
- 2 bedrooms, 1 bath
- Crawl space foundation

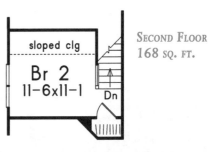

SECOND FLOOR
168 SQ. FT.

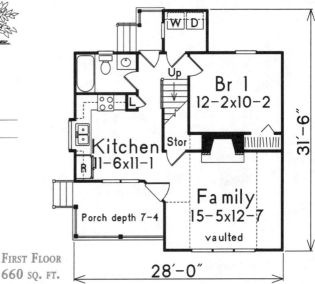

FIRST FLOOR
660 SQ. FT.

Open Layout
Ensures Easy Living

SPECIAL FEATURES

- 976 total square feet of living area
- Cozy front porch opens into large living room
- Convenient half bath is located on first floor
- All bedrooms are located on second floor for privacy
- Dining room has access to the outdoors
- 3 bedrooms, 1 1/2 baths
- Basement foundation

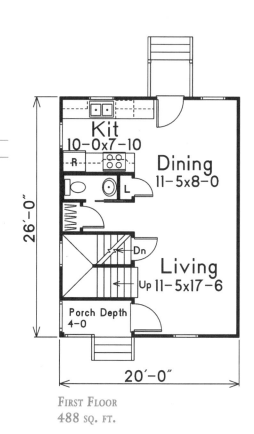

Kit
10-0x7-10

Dining
11-5x8-0

Living
Up 11-5x17-6

Dn

Porch Depth
4-0

26'-0"

20'-0"

FIRST FLOOR
488 SQ. FT.

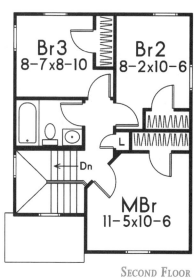

Br3
8-7x8-10

Br2
8-2x10-6

Dn
L

MBr
11-5x10-6

SECOND FLOOR
488 SQ. FT.

Plan #X22-15031

Three Car Garage Apartment

SECOND FLOOR

Dn
Deck

Br 2
10-0x11-0

Kit
10-6x
11-0

Din
9-8x11-3

Dn

Br 1
12-0x10-8

Living
20-9x14-0

Up

FIRST FLOOR

Garage
35-4x25-4

26'-0"

40'-0"

Up

SPECIAL FEATURES

- 1,040 total square feet
- Building height - 23'-0"
- Roof pitch - 5/12
- Ceiling height - 8'-0"
- Three 9' x 7' overhead doors
- 2 bedrooms, 1 bath
- Large rooms offer comfortable living with second floor laundry, ample cabinets and sliding doors to deck
- Complete list of materials

Plan #X22-15009

Sport Cabin

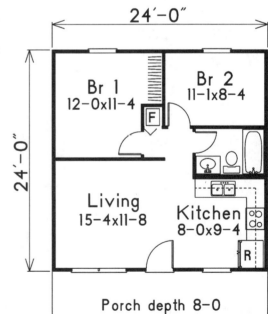

24'-0"

24'-0"

Br 1
12-0x11-4

Br 2
11-1x8-4

F

Living
15-4x11-8

Kitchen
8-0x9-4

R

Porch depth 8-0

SPECIAL FEATURES

- 576 total square feet
- Pier foundation
- Building height - 25'-6"
- Roof pitch - 6/12
- Ceiling height - 8'-0"
- 2 bedrooms, 1 bath
- Ideal for avid hunter or fisherman
- Complete list of materials
- Step-by-step instructions

Project Plans

Plan #X22-15032

Three Car Garage Apartment Cape Cod Style

SPECIAL FEATURES

- 813 total square feet
- Building height - 22'-0"
- Roof pitch - 12/12, 4.25/12
- Ceiling height - 8'-0"
- Three 9' x 7' overhead doors
- Studio, 1 bath
- Spacious studio apartment with kitchen and bath
- Perfect for recreation, in-laws or home office
- Complete list of materials

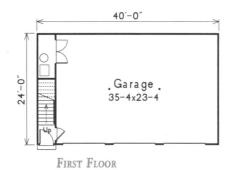

FIRST FLOOR

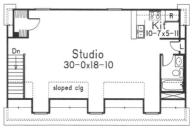

SECOND FLOOR

Project Plans

Plan #X22-15026

Two Car Garage Apartment With Gambrel Roof

SPECIAL FEATURES

- 604 square feet
- Building height - 21'-4"
- Roof pitch - 4/12, 12/4.75
- Ceiling height - 8'-0"
- Two 9' x 7' overhead doors
- Charming Dutch Colonial style
- Spacious studio provides extra storage space
- Complete list of materials
- Step-by-step instructions

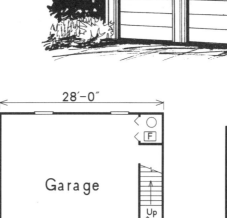

FIRST FLOOR

SECOND FLOOR

Plan #X22-15014

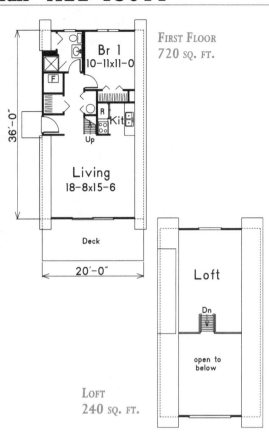

FIRST FLOOR
720 SQ. FT.

Br 1
10-11x11-0

F

Up

Kit

R

36'-0"

Living
18-8x15-6

Deck

20'-0"

Loft

Dn

open to
below

LOFT
240 SQ. FT.

A-Frame Cottage

SPECIAL FEATURES

- 960 square feet
- Pier foundation
- Building height - 22'-0"
- Roof pitch - 24/12
- 1 bedroom, 1 sleeping loft, 1 bath
- Open central living area is functional and spacious
- Complete list of materials
- Step-by-step instructions

Plan #X22-15017

Price Code P10

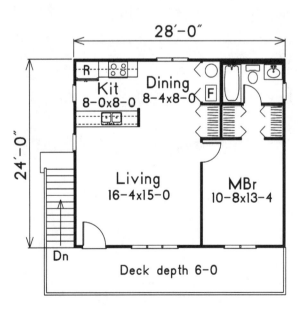

28'-0"

R

Kit
8-0x8-0

Dining
8-4x8-0

F

24'-0"

Living
16-4x15-0

MBr
10-8x13-4

Dn

Deck depth 6-0

Three Car Carport With Apartment

SPECIAL FEATURES

- 672 square feet
- Building height - 22'-0" with 8'-0" carport height
- Roof pitch - 4/12
- Apartment can double as vacation getaway
- 1 bedroom, 1 bath
- Complete list of materials
- Step-by-step instructions

Project Plans

Plan #X22-15506

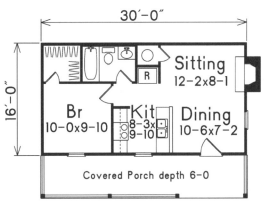

30'-0"

16'-0"

Sitting
12-2x8-1

Br
10-0x9-10

Kit
8-3x
9-10

Dining
10-6x7-2

R

Covered Porch depth 6-0

Exclusive Retreat

SPECIAL FEATURES

- 480 square feet
- Slab foundation
- Building height - 14'-2"
- Roof pitch - 6/12
- Ceiling height - 8'-0"
- 1 bedroom, 1 bath
- Cozy cabin includes large fireplace in sitting area with views into dining area
- Complete list of materials

Project Plans

Plan #X22-15028

Price Code P10

Two Car Garage Apartment Cape Code Style

SPECIAL FEATURES

- 566 square feet
- Building height - 22'-0"
- Roof pitch - 12/12, 4.5/12
- Ceiling heights-
  First Floor - 8'-0"
  Second Floor - 7'-7"
- Two 9' x 7' overhead doors
- Charming dormers add appeal to this design
- Comfortable open living area
- Complete list of materials
- Step-by-step instructions

FIRST FLOOR

28'-0"

24'-0"

Garage

Up

SECOND FLOOR

Dn

Studio
18-2x18-4

R

PROJECT PLANS ORDER FORM

**For fastest service, Call Toll-Free
1-800-DREAM HOME
(1-800-373-2646) day or night**

Three Easy Ways To Order

1. CALL toll free 1-800-373-2646 for credit card orders. MasterCard, Visa, Discover and American Express are accepted.
2. FAX your order to 1-314-770-2226.
3. MAIL the Order Form to:

   **HDA, Inc.
   4390 Green Ash Drive
   St. Louis, MO 63045**

QUESTIONS?
**Call Our Customer Service Number
314-770-2228**

ORDER FORM

Please send me -
PLAN NUMBER X22- _____

PRICE CODE _____ (see Plan Page)

Reproducible Masters (see chart at right) $ _____
Initial Set of Plans $ _____
Additional Plan Sets (see chart at right)
_____ (Qty) at $ _____ each $ _____

SUBTOTAL $ _____
SALES TAX (MO residents add 7%) $ _____
☐ Shipping / Handling (see chart at right) $ _____
(each additional set add $2.00 to shipping charges)

TOTAL ENCLOSED (US funds only) $ _____

☐ Enclosed is my check or money order payable to HDA, Inc. (Sorry, no COD's)

I hereby authorize HDA, Inc. to charge this purchase to my credit card account (check one):

☐ MasterCard ☐ VISA ☐ DISCOVER NOVUS ☐ AMERICAN EXPRESS Cards

Credit Card number _____

Expiration date _____

Signature _____

Name _____
(Please print or type)
Street Address _____
(Please **do not** use PO Box)
City _____

State _____ Zip _____

Daytime phone number (____) - _____

Thank you for your order!

110

◆ **Exchange Policies -** Since blueprints are printed in response to your order, we cannot honor requests for refunds. However, if for some reason you find that the plan you have purchased does not meet your requirements, you may exchange that plan for another plan in our collection. At the time of the exchange, you will be charged a processing fee of 25% of your original plan package price, plus the difference in price between the plan packages (if applicable) and the cost to ship the new plans to you.

Please note: Reproducible drawings can only be exchanged if the package is unopened, and exchanges are allowed only within 90 days of purchase.

◆ **Building Codes & Requirements -** At the time the construction drawings were prepared, every effort was made to ensure that these plans and specifications meet nationally recognized codes. Our plans conform to most national building codes. Because building codes vary from area to area, some drawing modifications and/or the assistance of a professional designer or architect may be necessary to comply with your local codes or to accommodate specific building site conditions. We advise you to consult with your local building official for information regarding codes governing your area.

BLUEPRINT PRICE SCHEDULE

Price Code	1-Set	Additional Sets	Reproducible Masters
P4	$19.95	$10.00	$69.95
P5	$24.95	$10.00	$74.95
P6	$29.95	$10.00	$79.95
P7	$49.95	$10.00	$99.95
P8	$74.95	$10.00	$124.95
P9	$109.95	$10.00	$159.95
P10	$145.95	$10.00	$195.95
P11	$169.95	$10.00	$219.95
P12	$194.95	$10.00	$244.95
P13	$225.00	$45.00	$440.00

**Plan prices guaranteed through December 31, 2003.
Please note that plans are not refundable.**

SHIPPING & HANDLING CHARGES
EACH ADDITIONAL SET ADD $2.00 TO SHIPPING CHARGES

U.S. SHIPPING
Regular (allow 7-10 business days) $5.95
Priority (allow 3-5 business days) $15.00
Express* (allow 1-2 business days) $25.00

CANADA SHIPPING
Standard (allow 8-12 business days) $15.00
Express* (allow 3-5 business days) $40.00

OVERSEAS SHIPPING/INTERNATIONAL
Call, fax, or e-mail (plans@hdainc.com) for shipping costs.

* For express delivery please call us by 11:00 a.m. CST

HOME PLANS INDEX

PLAN NUMBER	SQ. FT.	PRICE CODE	PAGE #	MAT. LIST	FAX-A-PLAN
X22-0101	1,039	AA	19	X	X
X22-0102	1,246	A	54	X	X
X22-0103	1,351	A	37	X	X
X22-0104	1,359	A	65	X	X
X22-0105	1,360	A	87	X	X
X22-0106	1,443	A	97	X	X
X22-0108	1,516	B	101	X	X
X22-0118	1,816	C	68	X	X
X22-0192	1,266	A	79	X	X
X22-0207	1,550	B	35	X	X
X22-0209	1,556	B	88	X	X
X22-0216	1,661	B	98	X	X
X22-0241	829	AAA	89	X	X
X22-0242	717	AAA	30	X	X
X22-0243	581	AAA	62	X	X
X22-0270	1,448	A	33	X	X
X22-0271	1,368	A	82	X	X
X22-0272	1,283	A	84	X	X
X22-0273	988	AA	21	X	X
X22-0274	1,020	AA	52	X	X
X22-0275	1,270	A	90	X	X
X22-0276	950	AA	61	X	X
X22-0277	1,127	AA	57	X	X
X22-0316	1,824	C	45	X	X
X22-0447	1,393	B	20	X	X
X22-0461	828	AAA	104	X	X
X22-0462	1,028	AA	57	X	X
X22-0474	654	AAA	51	X	X
X22-0475	1,711	B	13	X	X
X22-0476	576	AAA	92	X	X
X22-0477	1,140	AA	6	X	X
X22-0478	1,092	AA	53	X	X
X22-0479	1,294	A	12	X	X
X22-0484	1,403	A	11	X	X
X22-0493	976	AA	105	X	X
X22-0494	1,085	AA	73	X	X
X22-0495	987	AA	96	X	X
X22-0496	977	AA	63	X	X
X22-0498	954	AA	48	X	X
X22-0502	864	AAA	43	X	X
X22-0534	1,288	A	103	X	X
X22-0539	1,769	B	9	X	X
X22-0547	720	AAA	26	X	X
X22-0548	1,154	AA	70	X	X
X22-0549	1,230	A	40	X	X
X22-0582	800	AAA	89	X	X
X22-0650	1,020	AA	52	X	X
X22-0651	962	AA	64	X	X
X22-0653	1,563	B	56	X	X
X22-0655	632	AAA	8	X	X
X22-0657	914	AA	5	X	X
X22-0658	647	AAA	39	X	X
X22-0670	1,170	AA	26	X	X
X22-0680	1,432	A	60	X	X
X22-0681	1,660	B	29	X	X
X22-0683	1,426	A	34	X	X
X22-0692	1,339	A	22	X	X
X22-0693	1,013	AA	100	X	X
X22-0694	1,285	A	49	X	X
X22-0695	448	AAA	75	X	X
X22-0696	676	AAA	32	X	X
X22-0697	924	AA	92	X	X
X22-0698	1,143	AA	80	X	X
X22-0699	1,073	AA	72	X	X

PLAN NUMBER	SQ. FT.	PRICE CODE	PAGE #	MAT. LIST	FAX-A-PLAN
X22-0700	416	AAA	15	X	X
X22-0726	1,428	A	28	X	X
X22-0732	1,384	A	10	X	X
X22-0734	929	AA	64	X	X
X22-0737	902	AA	66	X	X
X22-0739	1,684	B	25	X	X
X22-0757	1,332	A	72	X	X
X22-0764	896	A	100	X	X
X22-0765	1,000	AA	44	X	X
X22-0766	990	AA	22	X	X
X22-0769	1,440	A	43	X	X
X22-0795	1,399	A	93	X	X
X22-0806	1,452	A	16	X	X
X22-0807	1,231	A	7	X	X
X22-0808	969	AA	27	X	X
X22-0809	1,084	AA	14	X	X
X22-0810	1,200	A	47	X	X
X22-0811	1,161	AA	58	X	X
X22-0813	888	AAA	81	X	X
X22-0814	1,169	AA	77	X	X
X22-1293	1,200	A	24	X	
X22-N005	960	AA	104	X	
X22-N006	1,209	A	95	X	
X22-N010	624	AAA	75	X	
X22-N015	1,275	A	17	X	
X22-N020	1,836	C	36	X	
X22-N026	1,026	AA	78	X	
X22-N027	1,312	A	86	X	
X22-N042	1,280	A	55	X	
X22-N048	1,272	A	59	X	
X22-N049	1,391	A	83	X	
X22-N057	1,211	A	42	X	
X22-N061	1,224	A	85	X	
X22-N063	1,299	A	41	X	
X22-N064	1,176	AA	69	X	
X22-N065	1,750	B	46	X	
X22-N084	2,652	E	74	X	
X22-N085	1,316	A	76	X	
X22-N087	784	AAA	80	X	
X22-N089	1,160	AA	94	X	
X22-N107	1,680	B	18	X	
X22-N109	1,806	C	102	X	
X22-N113	1,260	A	50	X	
X22-N114	792	AAA	39	X	
X22-N118	527	AAA	69	X	
X22-N119	1,200	A	91	X	
X22-N124	1,528	B	99	X	
X22-N127	1,344	A	71	X	
X22-N130	1,584	B	67	X	
X22-N131	733	AAA	44	X	
X22-N142	1,354	A	23	X	
X22-N145	618	AAA	32	X	
X22-N147	865	AAA	31	X	
X22-N149	1,332	A	38	X	

PROJECT PLANS

PLAN NUMBER	SQ. FT.	PRICE CODE	PAGE #
X22-15009	576	P10	106
X22-15014	960	P10	108
X22-15017	672	P10	108
X22-15026	604	P10	107
X22-15028	566	P10	109
X22-15031	1,040	P12	106
X22-15032	813	P12	107
X22-15506	480	P11	109

WHAT KIND OF PLAN PACKAGE DO YOU NEED?

Now that you've found the home you've been looking for, here are some suggestions on how to make your Dream Home a reality. To get started, order the type of plans that fit your particular situation.

Your Choices:

THE 1-SET STUDY PACKAGE - We offer a 1-set plan package so you can study your home in greater detail. This one set is considered a study set and is marked "not for construction". It is a copyright violation to reproduce blueprints.

THE MINIMUM 5-SET PACKAGE - If you're ready to start the construction process, this 5-set package is the minimum number of blueprint sets you will need. It will require keeping close track of each set so they can be used by multiple subcontractors and tradespeople.

THE STANDARD 8-SET PACKAGE - For best results in terms of cost, schedule and quality of construction, we recommend you order eight (or more) sets of blueprints. Besides one set for yourself, additional sets of blueprints will be required by your mortgage lender, local building department, general contractor and all subcontractors working on foundation, electrical, plumbing, heating/air conditioning, carpentry work, etc.

REPRODUCIBLE MASTERS - If you wish to make some minor design changes, you'll want to order reproducible masters. These drawings contain the same information as the blueprints but are printed on erasable and reproducible paper. This will allow your builder or a local design professional to make the necessary drawing changes without the major expense of redrawing the plans. This package also allows you to print as many copies of the modified plans as you need.

MIRROR REVERSE SETS - Plans can be printed in mirror reverse. These plans are useful when the house would fit your site better if all the rooms were on the opposite side than shown. They are simply a mirror image of the original drawings causing the lettering and dimensions to read backwards. Therefore, when ordering mirror reverse drawings, you must purchase at least one set of right reading plans.

Our Blueprint Packages Offer...

Quality plans for building your future, with extras that provide unsurpassed value, ensure good construction and long-term enjoyment.

A quality home - one that looks good, functions well, and provides years of enjoyment - is a product of many things - design, materials, craftsmanship. But it's also the result of outstanding blueprints - the actual plans and specifications that tell the builder exactly how to build your home.

And with our BLUEPRINT PACKAGES you get the absolute best. A complete set of blueprints is available for every design in this book. These "working drawings," are highly detailed, resulting in two key benefits:

■ Better understanding by the contractor of how to build your home, and...

■ More accurate construction estimates.

When you purchase one of our designs, you'll receive all of the BLUEPRINT components shown here - elevations, foundation plan, floor plans, sections, and details. Other helpful building aids are also available to help make your dream home a reality.

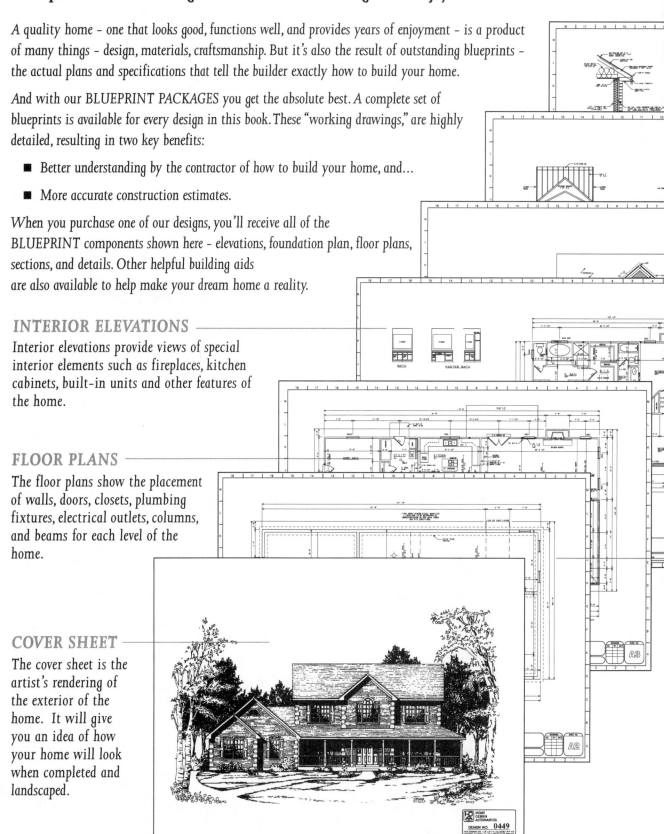

INTERIOR ELEVATIONS

Interior elevations provide views of special interior elements such as fireplaces, kitchen cabinets, built-in units and other features of the home.

FLOOR PLANS

The floor plans show the placement of walls, doors, closets, plumbing fixtures, electrical outlets, columns, and beams for each level of the home.

COVER SHEET

The cover sheet is the artist's rendering of the exterior of the home. It will give you an idea of how your home will look when completed and landscaped.

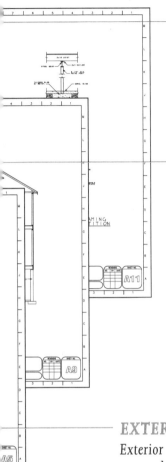

DETAILS

Details show how to construct certain components of your home, such as the roof system, stairs, deck, etc.

SECTIONS

Sections show detail views of the home or portions of the home as if it were sliced from the roof to the foundation. This sheet shows important areas such as load-bearing walls, stairs, joists, trusses and other structural elements, which are critical for proper construction.

EXTERIOR ELEVATIONS

Exterior elevations illustrate the front, rear and both sides of the house, with all details of exterior materials and the required dimensions.

FOUNDATION PLAN

The foundation plan shows the layout of the basement, crawl space, slab or pier foundation. All necessary notations and dimensions are included. See plan page for the foundation types included. If the home plan you choose does not have your desired foundation type, our Customer Service Representatives can advise you on how to customize your foundation to suit your specific needs or site conditions.

GENERAL BUILDING SPECIFICATIONS

This document outlines the technical requirements for proper construction such as the strength of materials, insulation ratings, allowable loading conditions, etc.

Other Helpful Building Aids...

Your Blueprint Package will contain the necessary construction information to build your home. We also offer the following products and services to save you time and money in the building process.

MATERIAL LIST

Material lists are available for many of the plans in this book. Each list gives you the quantity, dimensions and description of the building materials necessary to construct your home. You'll get faster and more accurate bids from your contractor while saving money by paying for only the materials you need. Refer to the Home plans Index on page 111 for availability. Check the order form on page 114 for pricing.

DETAIL PLAN PACKAGES:
Framing, Plumbing & Electrical Plan Packages

Three separate packages offer homebuilders details for constructing various foundations; numerous floor, wall and roof framing techniques; simple to complex residential wiring; sump and water softener hookups; plumbing connection methods; installation of septic systems and more. Each package includes three-dimensional illustrations and a glossary of terms. Purchase one or all three. Refer to the Home Plans Order form on page 114 for pricing. Note: These drawings do not pertain to a specific home plan. Cost: $20.00 each or all three for $40.00.

THE LEGAL KIT ™

Our Legal Kit provides contracts and legal forms to help protect you from the potential pitfalls inherent in the building process. The Kit supplies commonly used forms and contracts suitable for homeowners and builders. It can save you a considerable amount of time and help protect you and your assets during and after construction. Refer to the Home Plans Order form on page 114 for pricing.

EXPRESS DELIVERY

Most orders are processed within 24 hours of receipt. Please allow 7 working days for delivery. If you need to place a rush order, please call us by 11:00 a.m. CST and ask for express service (allow 1-2 business days).

TECHNICAL ASSISTANCE

If you have questions, call our technical support line at 1-314-770-2228 between 8:00 a.m. and 5:00 p.m. CST. Whether it involves design modifications or field assistance, our designers are extremely familiar with all of our designs and will be happy to help you. We want your home to be everything you expect it to be.

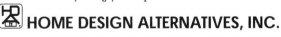

HOME DESIGN ALTERNATIVES, INC.

HOME PLANS ORDER FORM

How To Order

For fastest service, Call Toll-Free
1-800-DREAM HOME
(1-800-373-2646) day or night

Three Easy Ways To Order

1. CALL toll free 1-800-373-2646 for credit card orders. MasterCard, Visa, Discover and American Express are accepted.

2. FAX your order to 1-314-770-2226.

3. MAIL the Order Form to:

   HDA, Inc.
   4390 Green Ash Drive
   St. Louis, MO 63045

ORDER FORM

Please send me -

PLAN NUMBER X22- _____

PRICE CODE _____ (Index on page 111)

Specify Foundation Type - see plan page for availability
- ☐ Slab   ☐ Crawl space
- ☐ Basement   ☐ Walk-out basement
- ☐ Reproducible Masters $ _____
- ☐ Eight-Set Plan Package $ _____
- ☐ Five-Set Plan Package $ _____
- ☐ One-Set Study Package (no mirror reverse) $ _____
- ☐ Additional Plan Sets
    _____ (Qty.) at $45.00 each $ _____
- ☐ Print in Mirror Reverse
    _____ (Qty.) add $5.00 per set $ _____
- ☐ Material List (see chart at right) $ _____
- ☐ Legal Kit (see page 113) $ _____
- Detail Plan Packages: (see page 113)
    ☐ Framing ☐ Electrical ☐ Plumbing $ _____
                           SUBTOTAL $ _____
- SALES TAX (MO residents add 7%) $ _____
- ☐ Shipping / Handling (see chart at right) $ _____
    TOTAL ENCLOSED (US funds only) $ _____
    (Sorry no CODs)

I hereby authorize HDA, Inc. to charge this purchase to my credit card account (check one):

☐ MasterCard   ☐ VISA   ☐ DISCOVER NOVUS   ☐ AMERICAN EXPRESS Cards

Credit Card number _____

Expiration date _____

Signature _____

Name _____
(Please print or type)

Street Address _____
(Please do not use PO Box)

City _____

State _____ Zip _____

Daytime phone number (_____) - _____

I'm a ☐ Builder/Contractor   I ☐ have
      ☐ Homeowner   ☐ have not
      ☐ Renter   selected my
                                general contractor

Thank you for your order!

114

✂ IMPORTANT INFORMATION TO KNOW BEFORE YOUR ORDER

◆ **Exchange Policies -** Since blueprints are printed in response to your order, we cannot honor requests for refunds. However, if for some reason you find that the plan you have purchased does not meet your requirements, you may exchange that plan for another plan in our collection. At the time of the exchange, you will be charged a processing fee of 25% of your original plan package price, plus the difference in price between the plan packages (if applicable) and the cost to ship the new plans to you.

Please note: Reproducible drawings can only be exchanged if the package is unopened, and exchanges are allowed only within 90 days of purchase.

◆ **Building Codes & Requirements -** At the time the construction drawings were prepared, every effort was made to ensure that these plans and specifications meet nationally recognized codes. Our plans conform to most national building codes. Because building codes vary from area to area, some drawing modifications and/or the assistance of a professional designer or architect may be necessary to comply with your local codes or to accommodate specific building site conditions. We advise you to consult with your local building official for information regarding codes governing your area.

Questions? Call Our Customer Service Number
314-770-2228

BLUEPRINT PRICE SCHEDULE					BEST VALUE
Price Code	**1-Set**	*SAVE $110* **5-Sets**	*SAVE $200* **8-Sets**	**Material List***	**Reproducible Masters**
AAA	$225	$295	$340	$50	$440
AA	$275	$345	$390	$55	$490
A	$325	$395	$440	$60	$540
B	$375	$445	$490	$60	$590
C	$425	$495	$540	$65	$640
D	$475	$545	$590	$65	$690
E	$525	$595	$640	$70	$740
F	$575	$645	$690	$70	$790
G	$650	$720	$765	$75	$865
H	$755	$825	$870	$80	$970

Plan prices guaranteed through December 31, 2003.
Please note that plans are not refundable.

◆ **Additional Sets* -** Additional sets of the plan ordered are available for $45.00 each. Five-set, eight-set, and reproducible packages offer considerable savings.

◆ **Mirror Reverse Plans* -** Available for an additional $5.00 per set, these plans are simply a mirror image of the original drawings causing the dimensions & lettering to read backwards. Therefore, when ordering mirror reverse plans, you must purchase at least one set of right reading plans.

◆ **One-Set Study Package -** We offer a one-set plan package so you can study your home in detail. This one set is considered a study set and is marked "not for construction". It is a copyright violation to reproduce blueprints.

*Available only within 90 days after purchase of plan package or reproducible masters of same plan.

SHIPPING & HANDLING CHARGES

U.S. SHIPPING	1-4 Sets	5-7 Sets	8 Sets or Reproducibles
Regular *(allow 7-10 business days)*	$15.00	$17.50	$25.00
Priority *(allow 3-5 business days)*	$25.00	$30.00	$35.00
Express* *(allow 1-2 business days)*	$35.00	$40.00	$45.00

CANADA SHIPPING (to/from) - Plans with suffix DR & SH	1-4 Sets	5-7 Sets	8 Sets or Reproducibles
Standard *(allow 8-12 business days)*	$25.00	$30.00	$35.00
Express* *(allow 3-5 business days)*	$40.00	$40.00	$45.00

Overseas Shipping/International - Call, fax, or e-mail (plans@hdainc.com) for shipping costs.

* For express delivery please call us by 11:00 a.m. CST